DOGGETT DETERMINATION
Believing in Yourself to Create Success in Life and Business

RON E. DOGGETT
Retired Chairman, President & CEO
GoodMark Foods, Inc.
and its successful brand of Slim Jim meat snacks

with Karen Zelden

Foreword by Larry C. Farrell,
author, The New Entrepreneurial Age

Published and printed in the United States

Library of Congress Control Number: 2014913565
Zelden Writing Solutions, LLC, Apex, North Carolina

ISBN-13: 978-0692264355
ISBN-10: 0692264353

First Edition, 2014

Cover design by leesa brinkley graphic design, inc.

*Photos and Images: For authenticity, this book
includes some photos and images with original,
uneven and untouched borders.*

*This book chronicles the life story and experiences
of Ron E. Doggett, retired Chairman, President &
Chief Executive Officer, GoodMark Foods, Inc.,
as told from Ron's perspective based on his knowledge,
recollections and perceptions. Any inaccuracy or
omission is strictly inadvertent and unintentional.*

Ron, Austin, Minnesota, 1947

Ron, Grand Cayman Islands, 2004

Always bear in mind that your own resolution to succeed is more important than any one thing.

- Abraham Lincoln

This book chronicles the life story and experiences of Ron E. Doggett, retired Chairman, President & Chief Executive Officer, GoodMark Foods, Inc., as told from Ron's perspective based on his knowledge, recollections and perceptions.

Any inaccuracy or omission is strictly inadvertent and unintentional.

~

Photos and Images:

For authenticity, this book includes some photos and images with original, uneven and untouched borders.

Foreword

by Larry C. Farrell

I've known Ron Doggett since we were classmates at the Harvard Business School in the late seventies. Since then Ron has lived the great American entrepreneurial dream: He led the leveraged buyout of a tiny subsidiary of a giant bureaucracy, built that small business into an entrepreneurial powerhouse, and then sold it off to another giant bureaucracy for *five hundred times* more than his own, original cash investment! And, to top it off, he's just about the nicest, humblest, and most honest man you'll ever meet. My friend, Ron Doggett, is living proof that sometimes the good guys in business - and in life - do finish first!

Ron's record at GoodMark Foods, and its ubiquitous *Slim Jim* product, is well documented and truly remarkable. It actually provided a valuable case study for my own research and writing on great entrepreneurs. I titled his story *"The Amazing Odyssey of Ron Doggett."* He started his career as a financial manager at General Mills, the third largest food company in the United States. He then spearheaded an early example of a leveraged buyout of a small, money losing subsidiary of that huge company. The price on paper was $31 million, but over 99 percent was to be paid out of future revenues. Doggett and his three man team got the deal for just $200,000 in equity - which they borrowed from a local bank - because General Mills couldn't find anyone else to take the bleeding subsidiary off their hands. As CEO, Ron made the business profitable in just nine months and for the next 16 years had a compound revenue growth rate of 12 percent and a compound earnings growth rate of 19 percent. He then sold the company to ConAgra, the fourth biggest food company in the United States for a whopping $240 million. His entrepreneurial career, sandwiched between two giant bureaucracies, made him a rich man and gave him a unique perspective on the cultural divide between *Fortune 500* companies and an entrepreneurially driven business.

However, this book is about more than his amazing business career - it's about Ron Doggett the consummate good and generous citizen, the caring and honorable family man, and the wonderful friend to all who know him. One of Ron's greatest quotes about how to run a business is: *"The most successful businesses don't do anything new, exotic, or dramatic. They do very simple things - very well."* Even more importantly, this also turns out to be good advice about how to run your life; not always focusing on *"new, exotic or dramatic"* things but rather concentrating on doing *"very simple things - very well."* This of course turns out to be the more fundamental and more difficult challenge in life.

The following pages, wonderfully written by Karen Zelden, chronicle Ron Doggett's challenges and multi-faceted achievements. This telling of Ron's life-long "amazing odyssey" should stand as a model for us all in how to do those simple - but most important and most difficult things in life - very well.

Larry Farrell is the Founder & CEO of The Farrell Company, the world's leading firm for researching and teaching entrepreneurship. He's the author of several books, including his most recent, *The New Entrepreneurial Age* (2011). He resides with his wife Sylvia in Staunton, Virginia and Oak Creek Valley, Arizona.

Writer's Note

Throughout the many months that Ron Doggett and I collaborated to make his inspiring story come to life, a conversation between us repeated itself several times. As the chapters unfolded and I learned more about Ron's life and values which shaped his roles as husband, father, son, brother, friend, philanthropist, community leader and business success story, I told him that I just might write another book. This book would chronicle all of the life-altering lessons *I* learned from *his* experiences.

Without fail, Ron would chuckle or just smile and in a humble way uniquely his own tell me that the second book would not contain much content. He could not fathom how his experiences could have such impact.

Through professional circumstances, I came face-to-face for the first time with this wonderful man who would become a mentor. For nearly four years we worked with many others on a $20 million fundraising campaign to benefit children in our community. I would get to know Ron very well as our campaign chair and fundraising leader, less so on a personal level. A chance conversation where Ron mentioned a bucket list desire for many years to write his biography and my sharing with him my writing passion and experience, led to the story on the pages ahead.

Ron had modest but important goals for this book. He wanted to preserve his stories and lessons as a love letter to current and future generations of Doggett's. Hundreds of hours invested in research and interviews with Ron, his children, other family members, colleagues, friends, and business and community leaders convinced me that his story has the potential to resonate with - and impact - a much wider audience.

Through my formal interviews and informal conversations with Ron, our relationship grew. While we can measure his success in the tangibles of titles and possessions as with any CEO, it's the intangibles that really fascinate. It became clear to me from our discussions that his unwavering adherence to his core values guided his decisions thereby positively impacting his life.

Ron Doggett has succeeded most as a human being. As I talked with those who know Ron best, over and over again I heard *nice guys finish first* when describing him. The loosely knit network of admirers that comprise the unofficial 'Ron Doggett Admiration Society' transcend zip codes, socio-economic backgrounds, professions, ages and time zones. I now understand why, and have become a charter member myself. The *how* of his remarkable journey inspires even more than the *what*.

This important story really told itself, and I am honored that Ron trusted me to help him give it structure and a voice.

Over the past nearly eighty years of his life, the litany of Ron's successes and the many lessons he learned through overcoming adversity provide ample inspiration. Yet, if you take away from this book how Ron's commitment to his beliefs - shaped by Depression-era parents he respected and wanted to make proud - contributed to his personal and professional achievements, you will understand *Doggett Determination.*

Before working with Ron on this project, I respected him. Throughout our partnership, I grew to admire him. By its end, I developed a deep and abiding affection and appreciation for this decent, humble and ordinary man whose achievements in life and business are anything *but* ordinary.

Chances are that after reading *Doggett Determination*, you not only will grow to like, respect and admire Ron Doggett.

You may just grow to love him too.

Karen Zelden
2014

Acknowledgements

I have a blessed life.

I do not know the words to adequately express my gratitude and appreciation to you, my family, friends and colleagues. I thank you from the bottom of my heart for your confidence, encouragement and support.

I wish space permitted me to acknowledge each and every one of you by name. Please know that I would be nowhere without you.

Special thanks to:

God:

> With gratitude for all the blessings you have bestowed on my family and me. Through good and difficult times, my faith in you has sustained me.

Jeanette:

> My dear wife and partner, your love, inspiration and encouragement for over fifty years has meant everything to me. You supported me through thick and thin, and when I needed it most. I dedicate this book to you.

My children, Mark, Anne, Michael and Jane:

> I am very proud of the people you have become and the lives you lead. Along with your spouses, Kathryn, Ron, Libby and David and children Anna, Lauren, Kate, Ashley, Sarah, Ava, Mary Grace, Sean,

Christina, Emily and Edwin, you remind me every day what really matters in life.

I love you all.

My parents:

> Thank you for instilling in me *Doggett Determination* and all of the values that contributed to my personal and professional success. I miss you every day.

My family, friends and colleagues who contributed to this book:

> Words cannot express my gratitude for your support of this project. To those that urged me to write this book, participated in interviews and helped make it a reality, my heartfelt appreciation and thanks. It is a privilege for me to know you all.

> Special thanks to my sisters Janet Commers, Gwen Jordan, Shirley Patterson and Janeth Ranum; Bill Atkinson, Al Blalock, Paul Brunswick, Charlie Chewning, Al Colling, Tom D'Alonzo, Brenda Gibson, Kay Green, David Jessen, Jay Loftin, Kevin McCarthy, Henry Mitchell, Clint Neal, Tom Oxholm, Charles Re Corr, Father Mark Reamer, Billie Redmond, Walter Rogers, Bonnie Torgerson, Smedes York and Gil Zuckerman.

My GoodMark Foods family:

> I remain in awe of your talents, energy and what we accomplished together. Thank you.

Larry Farrell:

> Special thanks for your friendship over the years, and taking your valuable time to write my book's Foreword. It means the world to me.

Karen Zelden:

> My deepest appreciation for your friendship, guidance, and writing talent. Working with you to create this book was a joy.

Contents

l-r, Jane, Mark, Michael, Anne, Jeanette and
Ron Doggett, Deer Valley, Utah, 1994

Introduction

As a hard-working, fun-loving brother to four sisters growing up on a Minnesota farm in the 1930's and 1940's, I could not have predicted in my wildest dreams how my life would unfold.

Professionally, progressing from attending a one-room rural school to becoming Chairman, President and CEO of GoodMark Foods, Inc. (GoodMark) took me on a journey that few have the good fortune to navigate. Personally, I hit the jackpot when I married the love of my life, Jeanette, whose friendship, wisdom, support and partnership over the past fifty years contributed greatly to any professional success I achieved. Our four children, their spouses, eleven grandchildren, a large extended family and our circle of close friends remind me daily what really matters most. My professional success would mean nothing without them.

I am humbled and immensely grateful. I won the lottery in business and life.

Like most journeys worth taking, the unexpected fork in the road sometimes presented itself without warning giving me opportunities and decisions to make that tested me in ways unimagined.

I experienced times in my life of smooth progression as well as obstacles that many might have thought insurmountable. From an early age, I frequently found myself in the role of *underdog*.

During my career spent entirely at General Mills and GoodMark, I experienced soaring career highs and disappointing, potentially career-ending lows. On several occasions, various General Mills' bosses encouraged me to seek employment elsewhere. Promotions into leadership positions that I knew I had the talent, ambition and accomplishment to excel in passed me by. For many years, I felt stuck in roles for which I felt overqualified and underutilized.

For a variety of reasons explained in this book, I had faith in myself when others did not. I knew I could succeed as a senior leader. With my wife Jeanette's unwavering support, I decided to stay at General Mills rather than look for other employment. With determination, I made it my mission to excel, work hard and do my very best to prove my capabilities.

Then, a boss added unexpected insult to injury during one of my annual performance evaluations. He encouraged me to concentrate on doing my best at my current level because, as he said to me, *"you are not management material."* This wholesale dismissal of my abilities and potential made me angry, and put me on a determined path to prove that I could and would successfully lead.

Throughout it all, I believed in my potential. I would find a way to achieve as I knew I could.

I took great pride when after I became GoodMark CEO, this executive acknowledged he underestimated my leadership capabilities - and me. We became friendly. Years later, I was honored to deliver his eulogy.

General Mills' decision to sell GoodMark, which manufactured the snack food *Slim Jim*, presented the professional opportunity of a lifetime for me. I had *Doggett Determination* to mount a management buy-out of the company, and my partners and I accomplished this goal in May, 1982 when we completed the purchase for $31.5 million. Securing financing for the deal involved great personal risk for my colleagues, not to mention my family and me. Once again, Jeanette supported me 100% and, with her characteristic enthusiasm, told me to *"go for it."* I would hear those words from my wife many times throughout our life together.

The sixteen years that I had the privilege to lead GoodMark represent some of the happiest, exciting, challenging and rewarding years of my life. My opportunity had come to lead - and lead *my* way. Working with a talented team, we sought to create an inspired and motivated working environment. A culture that rewarded individual effort, great ideas, excellence and entrepreneurial spirit, where all shared in the company's success.

Our approach worked. GoodMark's talented employees took a company with declining sales and, in just over ten years, turned it into a business that *Forbes Magazine* ranked as #11 among the best 100 small companies in America. In 1998, we sold a profitable company to ConAgra for nearly $240 million, eight times the purchase price. At the time, I commented "[t]his agreement offers our shareholders excellent value." I still believe it.

Years later, I learned that a *New York Times* crossword puzzle included *Slim Jim* as one of its answers. I felt pride that our team's hard work had contributed to making it *that* well-known.

With great risk, comes the potential for both great reward and crashing defeat. Professionally, I was a late bloomer with the success I aspired to achieve occurring later in my career. When Jeanette and I 'went for it' and decided to participate in GoodMark's management buy-out, we literally put our financial future on the line. That decision, which we made after very careful consideration, and the hard work that followed allowed my family in recent years to enjoy the financial fruits of that labor.

However, it was not always the case. For many years, our family lived on a tight budget.

While my children had a front-row seat to see the ups and downs of my career and financial success, my grandchildren and future Doggett generations did not.

Like many, I have needed to correct my own life's path due to circumstances not of my choosing. As the saying goes, *life happens when you are busy making plans.* My wife's Alzheimer's Disease and breast cancer as well as my own Parkinson's Disease caused us to dramatically alter how we expected to live our retirement years. Yet, through my professional and personal trials, tribulations and successes, adhering to my basic core values has remained an important and comforting constant.

I write this book:

- To share the lessons I have learned along the way from the talented professionals with whom I have had the privilege to work. The accomplishments and success I have enjoyed in my professional career; on various boards of directors; and in my community and philanthropic activities, have come from working with a team.
- In the hopes that my grandchildren and future generations of Doggett's learn that success in life comes through hard work and resilience. Jeanette and I achieved our dreams that way, and they can too. Perhaps they will inherit our *Doggett Determination*.
- For the recent college graduate or experienced professional frustrated with his or her career path or perceived road

blocks to success. I hope my example instills confidence that victories come from believing in your abilities and not letting anyone derail or diminish you.

- For anyone who questions whether you can accomplish your career or life goals *and* stay true to your core values. My story emphasizes you can and should.

I also write this book as a special tribute and thank you to the employees and boards of directors who worked hard to establish a legacy of success at GoodMark from 1982-1998. I remain grateful to you and for what we accomplished together.

Ron Doggett
2014

My wife Jeanette (short hair) and me
celebrating my retirement, 1999

Chapter One

ABOUT HARD WORK

"You are not management material."

My family and me, Austin, Minnesota, circa 1945. My talented
mom made my sisters' dresses from poultry feed sacks!

It was June, 1972. At thirty-seven years old, I enjoyed a wonderful life. I had worked as a loyal and dedicated employee at General Mills for eleven years. Jeanette and I had a growing family of four healthy and happy children ranging in ages from three months to seven years old. We had relocated our family for my career three times taking us from Minnesota to Illinois to Pennsylvania to North Carolina. I wanted to spend my entire career with this corporate giant, and aspired to leadership opportunities that I felt matched my dedication, skills and passion for the company's products and services. Although I had experienced a few career bumps along the way, I thought I had navigated through those challenges and faced a bright future with a company I truly loved.

My annual performance evaluation that fateful June day changed everything. My boss telling me to focus on excelling as a staff accountant because, in his estimation, *'you are not management material'* rang in my ears as I left his office. I knew I had some decisions to make, as it had become crystal clear that my career aspirations did not align with this executive's perceptions of my abilities. Should I consider my options outside of General Mills and start over somewhere else, or should I work harder to change the misperceptions about my capabilities?

I chose to stay and work harder.

My boss could not have known that I had learned the value of hard work and tenacity many years earlier.

I came into the world during a snowstorm in December 1934 in Austin, Minnesota, a small farming community located about 100 miles south of Minneapolis and 170 miles north of Des Moines, Iowa. My father, Emil Day Doggett, and mother, Inez Cecilia Baldus, started their life together as husband and wife on June 15, 1931. They settled on a 160-acre dairy farm in Oakland, Minnesota, about eight miles from Austin. Growing up in a post-depression, small, rural community with few neighbors in close proximity, my four sisters, two older and two younger, became my closest friends and confidants.

As I understand it, my unique name, Ronnilee Emil, came from a compromise between my parents. My mother had a deep respect and admiration for her Uncle Leo, and wanted my name to somehow honor her uncle and my dad. My dad wanted to call me Ron, although why remains a mystery. Few people called me Ronnilee during my youth except an occasional teacher or classmate who teased me when hearing my unusual name. Most people followed my grandfather's lead and called me 'Sonny.'

I do not know its origin, but it stuck.

I must admit, I much preferred Sonny to Ronnilee. By high school, nearly everyone called me

Ronnie. In part because of the good-natured teasing about my 'feminine sounding' name I endured during my military service, I officially changed my name to Ron shortly after my discharge in 1956.

Hard work became an expectation of my existence for as long as I can remember. As a young child, I vividly recall my father coaxing me from my warm bed at 5:00 a.m. daily to help with farm chores for several hours before school started. On non-school days the early wake-up call continued and, during some periods of the year, I frequently worked twelve hours side-by-side with my dad. Our farm produced diverse cash crops including soy beans, oats and corn, and we raised chickens and other animals in addition to cows.

An endless *to do* list of necessary chores awaited me each day that required time management and a rigid adherence to a schedule. Working on our farm taught me many important skills that would serve me well in business. Farming effectively requires diligent planning and execution. Cows need milking at regular intervals and crops need harvesting at certain times. My dad, as my first boss, taught me the importance of discipline, prioritizing tasks to accomplish the most important ones first and time management.

I like to joke that I traded in 'sweat equity' during this period of my life.

I have met many hard workers over the years, yet very few people define work ethic like my dad. A strong, muscular guy, he demonstrated to my sisters and me by his actions that working hard and accomplishing matters in life. As a boy, I worshipped him and wanted to make him proud. I carry his first name, Emil, as my middle name, and that gives me tremendous pride. He had very high expectations for my performance and behavior, and wanted me to achieve at a higher level than my peers to reflect well both on me and our family. He lived by the principle that you should do any job properly the first time. 'Properly' to him pretty much meant perfection.

Work is healthy became the family motto, spoken by my dad nearly each day.

My first performance appraisals came from my father, with constructive feedback more likely than praise. He communicated his displeasure through words and looks, and rarely raised his voice. I worked hard so that when he inspected my work, I not only lived up to his expectations, I exceeded them. *I need to do this myself next time* as a critique from my dad made me doubly focused on getting the task right. I did whatever necessary to minimize hearing those words. Living up to my dad's high performance standards informed much of my youth. It bears repeating - I worked hard to make him proud and, most importantly, avoid disappointing him at all costs.

My dad instilled in me at a very early age an important lesson that has served me well during my life: *with a positive attitude, hard work and a clear plan, in the United States you can accomplish nearly anything.* He had little patience or tolerance for excuses. I learned to focus on what I could accomplish and spent little time or energy on that which I could not change. In high school, as an example, while I loved basketball and football, my small stature prevented me from playing in team sports. When I had a break from my farm chores, I focused on other athletic pursuits like hunting and fishing where I could excel. I learned the importance of adapting and focusing on *solutions* early in life. Worrying about things I could not change has never occupied much of my time, thanks to my dad.

My hard working father passed away in October 1978 at age 70, three-and-a-half years before our management buy-out of GoodMark occurred. I often wish that he could have witnessed that achievement, which his guidance helped make possible. I know he would have been proud of his only son. *Work is healthy, Dad.*

While my relationship with my father taught me the value of discipline, hard work, achievement, prioritizing, excellence, and pride in a job well done, my relationship with my mom equally informed the man and leader I grew to become. My mother also personified hard work, as well as empathy, patience, kindness and compassion. Hugs and affection generally came from Mom. A devout Catholic, she balanced her kind and sweet disposition with intolerance for lying, laziness or swearing from any of her children. Discipline sometimes came in the form of a threat to have your mouth washed out with soap, a common punishment back then but one not frequently used today. I assure you that this generally corrected the unacceptable behavior rather quickly!

While my father managed our farm, my mother served as permanent CEO of our household with a dizzying array of tasks that awaited her and my sisters each day. She lived by the three 'C's - cleaning, cooking and canning. Fruit trees on our farm provided an endless supply of bounty for the canning bees that Mom sometimes hosted with our neighbors. My sisters and I looked forward to baking day when the smell of ginger cookies, rolls, donuts and the pastry *kolache*, a Doggett family favorite, filled the air. I learned the value of positive reinforcement from my mother, as she rewarded my siblings' and my good behavior with batter tastings from whatever sweet concoction's scent would soon fill the air and occupy space in our oven. I liked the batter as much if not more than the finished product!

Our household ran as well as any successful business thanks to my mom's skills in organization, planning, priority-setting and patience. I can remember many a squabble with my sisters where my mother patiently listened to all sides of the story before deciding on the right course of action or, as we got older, encouraging us to problem-solve without her input. This valuable lesson has served me well over the years in both my personal and professional life.

My mother's resourcefulness often astounded me. While hard work on the farm and inside our home existed in plentiful supply, money did not during most of my youth. My mother's ability to turn poultry sacks into clothing for her children became legendary. Piping hot hard boiled eggs in our coat pockets helped to keep our hands warm during the bitterly cold Minnesota winters. Some years, Santa Claus brought our family only fruit for Christmas, but my mother did her best to make holidays as joyous as possible no matter our financial circumstances. Of course, the hard work required to sustain a dairy farm does not stop for holidays, and a laundry list of chores awaited us 365 days a year. They *always* came first before any fun or celebration.

Farming also teaches you constructive ways to deal with mistakes and setbacks, whether beyond your control or self-imposed. Unexpected weather conditions like drought, floods and heat; unwelcome and uninvited bugs and pests that can destroy crops; animal disease; economic conditions; and a whole host of other variables impacted our farm's productivity and our livelihood from year-to-year. Witnessing first-hand the life cycle of growth-to-sale taught me the basic economic principle of supply and demand, and the difficulty of accurately predicting what may or may not sell in any given year.

Throughout their ups and downs, my parents worked as a team and challenges only made them try harder. Living through the Depression informed their values and determination; it taught them to appreciate the results of their hard work and efforts. They never gave up. Their example taught me that how you *respond* to adversity matters more than the challenge itself.

Their belief in both the importance of effort and my capabilities served me well after that fateful day in June 1972 when I made the decision to stay at General Mills and work even harder to prove myself.

My mother, who passed away just before her 90th birthday in 1996, lived to see her only son become the Chief Executive Officer of an American company. This ranks as one of my proudest moments, and a testament to the value of hard work instilled in me by my humble and high achieving parents.

Inez and Emil Doggett, Austin, Minnesota, 1952

Chapter Two

ABOUT LEARNING

"I frequently rode a pony to school."

Riding Nettie, circa 1945

The Early Years

My formal education beginning in first grade at age six started *Lucky*.

With my pony, *Lucky*, that is.

My life-long love of learning officially began in 1940 in a one-room schoolhouse, Lugg School District 95 in Oakland, Minnesota, about one-and-a-half miles from our family farm. Each year, between ten and sixteen children total in grades one through eight shared this school. It boasted a large pot-belly stove for heat and not one, but *two*, outhouses. My sisters attended as well, and the Doggett kids comprised half of the school population some years!

Attending Lugg also represented the first time in my life that I would begin learning from adults other than my mom, dad and other family members. While I loved our farm and working side-by-side with my dad, I enjoyed the respite that school provided. The opportunity to spend a significant amount of time with other kids not related to me was a bonus and helped me develop socially.

I had many teachers during my seven years at Lugg, and Mrs. Callahan stands out as one of my favorites. I remember to this day her infectious optimism and passion for teaching. I loved going to school, in large part because she instilled in me at an early age an enthusiasm for learning. She made

English, arithmetic and history fun. The more I learned, the more I wanted to know.

The start of my formal education coincided with dramatic events on the world stage, namely World War II. I learned about cities and countries that existed far away from the boundaries of our small Minnesota town. Little did I know that as a man, I would travel to many of the places that I first heard about all those years earlier.

Lucky (my favorite) or another family pony, *Nettie,* got me to and from school most days. I loved riding and spending time with our horses. During the cold and snowy winter months, cross-country skiing or walking did the job.

During my years at Lugg I proudly won a local spelling bee, yet failed to win the county contest when I advanced. I demonstrated a competitive streak early, and really wanted to win that second challenge. My parents, however, expressed great pride that not only did I win one match, I tried hard in the second even though I did not achieve the desired result.

Although disappointed with my performance, this provided me with an important early lesson to celebrate both results and effort; always do your best; and learn from your mistakes.

Lugg School, circa 1945

High School

Parents generally hope that their children's success will leapfrog their own, and mine were no exception.

My parents valued education, in partnership with a strong faith rooted in Catholicism, as two necessary ingredients in the recipe of life. This especially mattered to my father who had to leave school before graduating to begin working on the farm. (He proudly earned his high school diploma later in life.)

While we had a good public high school in our community and could have attended it tuition-free, my mother really wanted my sisters and me to attend private Catholic high school. So, attend Pacelli High School in Austin, Minnesota we did.

Although they tried to shield us, I recall their personal sacrifices to make that dream a reality. To say they were determined might be an understatement; paying for our high school education often came first before other important family expenses like insurance and farm repairs. My mom and dad scrimped, saved and frequently incurred debt so their children could get ahead in life.

Although I did not realize it at the time, upon reflection, my real education came from seeing how their goal-setting, planning, sacrifice and execution helped them achieve their objectives.

This lesson would serve me well throughout my adult life.

I experienced many 'firsts' during my high school years, and some of the most life-altering had nothing to do with academics. Living in the somewhat insular world of a small farm community did not prepare me adequately for what awaited me. Our high school included students from all walks of life and financial means. Students from wealthy backgrounds wearing expensive clothes and driving shiny new cars attended class side-by-side with those of us of more modest means.

I also learned that the city kids' experiences differed greatly from the country kids like me. Who knew that not everyone gets up at 5:00 a.m. to milk cows or rides a horse to get from one place to another? Quite unexpectedly, my high school experience exposed me for the first time to the knowledge that the world contained differences and, with those differences, *options*. I always thought I would follow in my parents' footsteps and continue with our family's farming tradition. High school planted the first seeds of possibility beyond farming that I would sow years later.

I remember Pacelli fondly, a place where I excelled academically and socially. Still, kids can be brutal and I took my fair share of teasing for my dress, small stature and country lifestyle. Unlike many of my classmates, the end of my school day generally meant more hours of work tending to farm animals, harvesting crops or completing any number of special projects. Rather than feeling diminished by the differences, they fueled my competitive spirit. I sought to prove to myself and others through hard work that I had the same capabilities as someone who, through an accident of birth, could afford more. I learned to focus on my strengths and what I had the control to positively impact. Academic success leveled the playing field, allowed me to compete and helped me earn my peers' respect.

Prejudice became a part of my consciousness for the first time during my high school years. I learned that some people pre-judge before ever getting to know you. As an example, I had more than one experience where fathers did not want their daughters to date me. How do I know this? They told their daughters - and me! One father, who knew little about me other than my address, communicated in the strongest possible terms that his daughter deserved better than a Catholic farm boy who he *knew* would not succeed in life. Not surprisingly, a relationship between his daughter and me never had a chance.

The hurt and disappointment I felt as a teenager eventually gave way to determination. I would prove to everyone including myself that attitude, drive, hard work and commitment matter. I planned to prove these fathers wrong.

Throughout my personal and professional life, I have tried to remember the unfairness of judging a 'book by its cover' and to give people a chance even when I have an initial unfavorable impression. I often have thought that starting out my life as an underdog undervalued by many actually was a gift. Unflattering opinions by others, including my *you are not management material* boss at General Mills, produced in me the same determination to prove them wrong as I felt in high school all those years ago. I learned to identify my strengths and focus on developing those to the very best of my ability. I also learned that believing in myself matters far more than what others think about me.

Graduating from Pacelli in June 1952 on the *honor roll* made my parents very proud. It also made *me* proud. It served as one of the first times in my life where I set a goal and achieved it. I made a decision to succeed - and followed through.

The 'dark horse' role would become a recurring theme throughout my life. It served me well, and propelled me to accomplish.

Ironically, six years later in 1958, a beautiful, charming young woman named Jeanette Reinartz also would graduate from Pacelli. Although we did not know each other in high school, Pacelli would become one of the many things that my future wife and I would find we have in common.

The School of Hard Knocks

Now what?
That answer did not come easily.

For eighteen years, I had led a fairly structured life dictated by the guidance and expectations of my parents, priests, nuns and teachers. Farm chores, church and schoolwork consumed a large percentage of my time and left me with a game plan for my day-to-day existence created *for* me, not *by* me.

With high school diploma now in hand, big changes occurred for which I had not adequately prepared. It thrust me into a new world of endless possibilities dictated now by my choices. I grew up expecting to live my life in Minnesota following in my father's footsteps as a farmer. With academic success and the broadened horizons that high school gave me, I began to realize that perhaps options existed for me beyond our farming community.

Before the milestones of graduation and turning eighteen years old occurred, I began to have doubts about becoming a farmer. I had just one small problem; I did not have a Plan B. I loved achieving academically, but did not consider college seriously. Even if I had wanted to attend, the financial resources to do so eluded me.

Unsure of my life's direction, I decided to try farming as a profession. I leased some land with my dad and for the next two-and-one-half years gave it a go. I quickly became restless. I had back then - and continue to have - enormous respect and appreciation for the important work that farmers do every day. Yet, as time progressed, my doubts about farming as my career got stronger.

As a child, I enjoyed working side-by-side with my dad. As a young man, I quickly learned the difficulties of making a living on a farm. I came to the realization that while I did not want to disappoint my father, I yearned to see what the world had to offer. Attending college like many of my Pacelli friends became a strong desire, although figuring out a way to pay for it proved more challenging. I did not see a clear path to turn my dream into a reality.

During this time, largely from immaturity and frustration, I also made some poor personal choices. With many of my high school friends in college or the military, I made some questionable new friends who seemed without goals and ambition. I stayed out too late to perform at my best on the farm. I focused on casual dating and accumulating material possessions, without much concern for my future.

If I ever had a rebellious phase in my life, this was it. My change in behavior worried my parents. I acted out. In an effort to find some direction and an outlet for my frustration, I began amateur boxing. Although I did not stick with it long-term, the discipline and focus necessary to train and compete helped get me back on track.

In October, 1954, the opportunity I sought to continue my education presented itself when I least expected it. I learned that the United States Army actively sought new recruits; they would provide tuition support for anyone who volunteered for service by December 31, 1954! Not only had I found a solution to fund my college tuition, but I also would experience life beyond the only place I had ever known.

One month after my 21st birthday, I enlisted in the United States Army. I left Oakland, Minnesota with my parents' support to report for duty as Private Doggett on January 5, 1955. I could not have realized at the time how important the decision to enlist for military service would become for my professional future. Farming became an irretrievably closed chapter. To quote Julius Caesar, *the die was cast.*

Serving My Country

If asked to select the one pivotal moment that changed the trajectory of my life, my decision to enter the U.S. Army most certainly would be in contention. My twenty-one months of military service not only helped me mature, it gave me the focus and discipline that I desperately needed. Unlike boxing, I could not just quit. It straightened out my life and gave me direction. It also made me more convinced than ever that college would help me achieve my as yet undetermined professional goals.

My initial weeks in the military exposed me to a whirlwind of new experiences in places that I had never even heard of, much less visited, before. Eight weeks of basic training at Fort Leonard Wood, Missouri and Camp Chaffee, Arkansas set the stage for what military service would hold in store for me. Suddenly, others dictated how I would spend each day, from rising in the morning to lights out at night and every activity in between.

Life on a farm prepared me well for my day-to-day existence, with structure defining nearly all activities. We rose between 4:00 and 6:00 a.m., followed by a day prescribed by our superior officers that included military training, exercise and work in equal parts. Tardiness or absenteeism resulted in punishment which, thankfully, I did not experience during my military career. To this day, punctuality remains very important to me.

Achieving in the business world also requires discipline, and the Army instilled that in me right from the beginning.

After basic training, Fort Bliss in El Paso, Texas would become a dominant part of my military experience and would set the stage for my future career in accounting. Each soldier takes tests to determine their skills and aptitude. This leads to a MOS (Military Occupational Specialty) assignment, essentially your job. As a private assigned to Headquarters Commandant, my MOS involved keeping the books and doing office work. I loved the tasks, trust and responsibility given to me by my superior officers. It would become one of my first experiences with accomplishing a skill that could help me get a job in the business world.

Fort Bliss also gave me the opportunity to take my first college course - in business law. I loved it, and it only reinforced my strong desire to get my degree. Slowly, the pieces began to fall into place that led me down the right professional path.

I remember most the diverse people that I met in the service; many helped inform who I wanted to become as an adult. I admired the career military professionals - my superior officers - who displayed intelligence, discipline, goal-setting, and structure. Although I did not engage in combat, witnessing the toll on soldiers who had fought left a lasting impression on me. I admired their courage and bravery.

I also encountered people that I knew I did not want to become. Witnessing poor performance, mediocrity and a lack of discipline by some instilled in me a strong desire to surround myself with motivated, high performance individuals; in short, *winners*. In the military, like business and life, achievement matters.

Although I thrived in the Army and learned many important skills that served me well throughout my life, I never considered making it my career. The chain-of-command structure and rigid adherence to rules at all costs did not appeal to me long-term. I wanted to control my own destiny and ultimately direct, not be directed. My entrepreneurial leanings surfaced early.

On October 11, 1956, I received an honorable discharge from the Army. I finally would realize my aspirations to attend college. I could not wait to get started.

College

My college career, not to mention my life, nearly ended before it really began.

In late October 1956, I returned home to Minnesota and excitedly registered for courses at Austin Community College (ACC). The semester had begun several weeks earlier, but I wanted to start as soon as possible. I hastily followed ill-advised guidance to both start mid-semester, and take courses like Calculus and Chemistry not required for my desired degree in Business. I struggled more than I expected with re-entry back into the civilian world and course work not really in my area of interest or competency. Starting the semester late also resulted in my never catching up to the other students in my classes. I fell behind, and worried that college might not be for me after all.

Not long after enrolling at ACC, two friends and I traveled by car thirty-five miles to Rochester, Minnesota for a triple date on a snowy, bitterly cold winter night. With bravado, we decided that a little blizzard would not deter us. Plus, I wanted to show off my brand new Oldsmobile. After an enjoyable evening and dropping our dates safely off at home, we began the drive back to Austin well after midnight but never made it. I lost control of my car on an icy road. We struck a bridge post, careened over a creek and, after rolling over one complete turn, what was left of my car came to rest upright on the creek's edge. Seatbelts and other automobile safety features that we take for granted today were not commonly used back then.

Miraculously, all three of us lived but we sustained serious injuries that kept us hospitalized and recovering for several weeks. We were very lucky - and we knew it. I have no doubt that God watched over us that evening. Our dates already safely at home before the accident occurred gave me some comfort. No question, the incident scared me.

My convalescence gave me the opportunity to plan for my return to college. I wanted to succeed. I returned to ACC nearly a year after the accident in the Fall, 1957, and graduated in the Summer, 1959 with a two-year degree. I transferred to Mankato State College in Mankato, Minnesota (Minnesota State University today) and happily graduated in April, 1961 with a double major in Economics and Business Administration. Needless to say, my graduating made my parents very proud.

At twenty-six years old and with a few detours along the way, at long last I had earned my college degree.

The same month that I graduated, General Mills hired me as an internal auditor. My business career had begun.

Harvard Business School

Throughout my career and life, I have remained passionate about learning from others. As a leader, I never felt that I had a monopoly on all the good ideas. Far from it! Openness to fresh perspectives, different strategies, leadership styles and approaches to problem solving (and business in general) has many benefits. It facilitates personal growth, prevents stagnation and encourages team professional success.

I have witnessed this over and over again. I believe this approach contributed to GoodMark's success during my tenure as CEO.

Sometimes, great opportunities can come at inopportune times but are worth the short-term sacrifice and commitment for long-term gain. In the summer of 1979, eighteen years after beginning my career with General Mills, my boss nominated me to attend Harvard Business School's Advanced Management Program (AMP). Founded in 1945, this program provides intensive training to turn managers into visionary, global leaders.

I was honored to receive the nomination, and excited about the potential. I knew that attending certainly would enhance my resume and leadership opportunities. It also would mean that for seven weeks in the summers of 1979 and 1980, I would attend school in Boston, Massachusetts leaving Jeanette to care for our four children alone. Without my wife's support, I could not have attended.

Jeanette enthusiastically gave me the go-ahead. I took pleasure sharing the experiences from this outstanding program with her during our daily conversations. Completing AMP did enhance my career, which benefitted our family. Not only did I learn new skills and refine existing ones, but I had exposure to and developed relationships with business leaders from around the world. Several remain friends and associates to this day.

Through attending this program, perhaps most importantly, I gained confidence that I had the ability to run a large company. I felt energized and inspired to apply what I learned in my position at General Mills. Although I did not realize it in the summer of 1980 when I completed this education, less than two years later the opportunity of a lifetime to buy a company would present itself.

I would be ready.

Private Ronnilee Doggett

Chapter Three

ABOUT DETERMINATION and DEDICATION

"You might want to look for another job."

My first attempt in business actually started during my college years. An opportunity presented itself for me to help develop a small shopping center in southern Minnesota. I had saved some money while in the Army, and excitedly invested it in this project. I probably should not have been surprised when less than two years later the project failed, although I was very disappointed. In hindsight, my partners and I knew very little about shopping mall development. My desire to work as a 'businessman' coupled with my entrepreneurial nature, energy and, quite frankly, immaturity and inexperience, overrode approaching this project with caution and due diligence.

Although I lost my financial investment, I gained significant experience that would serve me well in business particularly when the chance to purchase GoodMark years later presented itself. Knowing your product or service inside and out would become one of the most important of those lessons. Like any entrepreneur, I also learned that great risk can lead to great reward. Although disappointed with the result, I felt energized by the experience. My business career had begun.

With the shopping mall's failure, I actively sought to complete my college education and pursue a more traditional corporate position. I thought I had caught the brass ring in April 1961 when General Mills, a well-known and respected company, hired me a few months past my twenty-sixth birthday. My many years of military service, college, hard work and entrepreneurial business experience finally had paid off. Virtually everyone I knew had heard of General Mills, and I now could proudly count myself as an employee. I again had made my family proud. I was ecstatic.

I envisioned a career at General Mills with many possibilities for growth and success. I thought my initial position as an internal auditor would lead me straight up the corporate ladder. I believed in my abilities, and knew that I had the work ethic and drive to succeed.

I would learn over the next twenty years, however, that despite your best efforts things don't always go according to plan.

My first few years with the company did exceed my expectations. As an auditor, my work on behalf of the company took me all over the United States and Canada. Each audit could take weeks and sometimes months, and I became well-known by hotel employees all over North America. When Jeanette became my wife in June 1962, she accompanied me for the first nineteen months of our marriage. We had a wonderful time. We met interesting people and experienced places that we never thought we would see. We lived in close enough proximity to our families in Minnesota that we saw them frequently. I worked hard, and thoroughly enjoyed my job and the travel.

During my initial years with General Mills, I learned a great deal about corporate culture and politics, as well as the technical aspects of my job.

I soaked up as much information as I could about our company in the hopes of securing a promotion early in my tenure. I was in every way a 'company man.'

That first promotion came three-and-one-half years later, in November 1964. Jeanette, our newborn son Mark and I moved to Chicago so that I could become an assistant office manager of a large General Mills-owned grocery products plant. By the time we had three children, Mark, Anne and Michael, I had become office manager of the same plant. Although we enjoyed living in Chicago, career-wise, I had become restless with my job. The time to pursue my next position within General Mills had arrived.

That opportunity came in August 1967, but required that I move my family from Chicago to Philadelphia. General Mills had acquired a company that manufactured the meat-stick snack food *Slim Jim*, and a vice president and chief financial officer position for this business had presented itself. I enthusiastically interviewed for this job, believing that it would provide me with a terrific chance to move my career forward. After all, neither vice president nor CFO opportunities come along every day. I also thought it a pretty big longshot, as it would represent a significant step in my career.

Jeanette and I celebrated in grand style when I learned the news that I got the job! I could not believe my good fortune. I was elated.

Little did I know at the time that accepting this position, which I thought would advance my career at General Mills, set me on a path that nearly ended it several times. I would learn months later that they hired me for what seemed like a significant promotion with a fancy title because they could find no one else to take the job. I soon would learn why.

In 1967, General Mills purchased Cherry-Levis, Co., which included the product *Slim Jim*, from Adolph Levis, a Philadelphia entrepreneur who made his living selling food products to delicatessens. It is reported that in 1928, Levis capitalized on an expanding customer appetite for processed meats like bologna and pepperoni and created a small dried sausage that he could sell. The story goes that he characterized his invention 'elegant,' personally designed the product's top hat and cane branding emblem, and named the product *Slim Jim*, which it retains to this very day.

The acquired business became Slim Jim, Inc., a division of General Mills, Inc. As with many acquisitions, General Mills retained Levis to run the business with a goal of ensuring a smooth transition. From my perspective, it did not go as planned. In accepting this position, I worked for Levis. Although he willingly sold his business to General Mills and reportedly profited handsomely, to me, he acted as though he still owned it. In dealings with him, I felt like the enemy.

In my view, his style clashed with the General Mills culture. I frequently had to work from home; when coming to the office, my General Mills colleagues and I sometimes found the office doors locked or we were summarily dismissed during the work day. Needless to say, my first year with this business unit did not go smoothly.

The location of the plant in an area with significant crime also presented some challenges. I unfortunately learned this the hard way. Within a few weeks of starting my new job, a gang of young men descended on me from the darkness as I walked to my car after a long work day, and began beating and mugging me. While I fortunately escaped and re-entered the plant bruised and bloodied but not seriously harmed, I witnessed them destroy my car with large concrete blocks.

As I watched helplessly, I truly thought that I had made a big mistake in taking this position and uprooting my family. Was working for a new division of General Mills whose claim to fame was a meat-stick snack food really worth it? Was having a fancy title without the level of real responsibility that I hoped would accompany it helpful to me in achieving my long-term career goals?

The answer would prove to be a resounding *yes*. At the time, my difficult working conditions coupled with watching a group of angry thugs destroy my car would have led me to a very different conclusion.

As I had accepted this assignment, I wanted to prove that as a dedicated General Mills employee I could help make this new business successful.

Thankfully, shortly after my mugging the company moved our plant and offices to a safer area of Philadelphia. I dedicated myself to learning as much as I could about the *Slim Jim* products and our division to make my best contribution. I began to enjoy my job more, and determinedly decided to give my all to this position to become ready for my next opportunity. I wanted my next role to include leading people.

In 1968, Levis' association with General Mills ended. I hoped his replacement would come from our company's leadership ranks to encourage a smoother transition for this new division into the company's culture. Instead, a General Mills' employee from another division - someone without executive leadership experience - was selected to take over. The decision mystified me, then and now. We learned that the new boss had attended a well-known business school. Did that perhaps contribute to management hoping he would bring forward some fresh ideas leading to our division's success?

Little did I know at the time that decisions made during this period would put me in a professionally vulnerable position that nearly cost me both my career at General Mills and reputation.

One such decision, not discussed with me before implementation, involved changing our practices to count product shipped to General Mills warehouses as *sales* (instead of *inventory*) prior to fulfilling orders for customers. Simply stated, this resulted in overstating our sales and performance.

Who specifically made that decision - does not really matter for this story. What does is how I felt when I learned about it and how I responded. I was angry to say the least. I strenuously objected from both an accounting and business perspective. It caused me many sleepless nights. I was told that General Mills had approved this practice, which I found surprising. If I had taken it further, I stood a strong chance of losing my job.

I did not. In hindsight, I wish I had.

My instincts proved correct. A few months later, General Mills learned what had occurred and heads rolled. Although I was not implicated in conceiving or implementing this practice, my competence and performance was called into question. I was held responsible for failing to control the situation. My reputation took a hit. They did not fire me, but strongly suggested that I seek employment outside the company. My career and dreams to advance with a company that I loved suffered a near-fatal blow.

I had a choice to make. Do I go as strongly suggested or do I try to stay?

I had invested over seven years in my career at General Mills, a company I loved. Today, loyalty between organizations and their employees has become nearly non-existent and changing jobs frequently, the norm. However, I worked in the generation who frequently retired with the gold watch after working for one organization their entire careers. I felt an enormous amount of dedication to this company. General Mills gave this farm boy the chance to achieve my dream of working in the business world. I felt gratitude.

I also had great determination and belief in my abilities. I strongly felt that with hard work and time, I could recover and prove to myself and my bosses that I had what it took to advance.

Leaving the company as suggested would leave a blemish on my record. An asterisk would appear next to my name and my reputation. I would leave *defeated* and as a *quitter*. Neither word applied to me, and I certainly did not want anyone else to think of me that way. If I ever left General Mills, I wanted to do so for the right reason - a great opportunity.

Fortunately, I also had influential colleagues who believed in me. All organizations have politics. Understanding them can mean the difference between success and unemployment. I cannot underscore the importance of cultivating mentors and advocates throughout your career who can help you develop professionally and navigate through difficult situations if needed. I thankfully had them during this very challenging period, and gratefully appreciated their support.

With the help of my mentors who advocated on my behalf and after passing (to General Mills' satisfaction) a battery of tests similar to Myers Briggs and other career assessments of today, I was allowed to keep my position. I decided to stay. I knew that my career had suffered a significant setback, but determinedly embarked on the journey to repair the damage and move forward.

The next four years of my career, from 1968-1972, would prove more challenging than I could have imagined. I had no idea how difficult my career rehabilitation would become.

In early 1969, a decision was made to move our division's corporate offices from Philadelphia to Raleigh. Our new division president called me into his office and wasted no time in telling me that he had hired a new corporate controller from outside our division. He went on to say that he would not need me in my current position and I should not plan to move to Raleigh. He strongly encouraged me to seek employment elsewhere.

In no uncertain terms, I knew where I stood. This time, I thought my career at General Mills had ended. I felt disappointed that I would not have the ability to prove myself to the new leadership team. I did not want to leave defeated, but it appeared that I had no options left.

The new controller convinced the president on the merits of having me remain with the division to ensure a smooth transition. Although they already had hired an assistant controller, I received an offer to become the *second* assistant controller with a significant reduction in pay and a very small relocation allowance.

To be honest, this career setback did unnerve me. I felt humiliated. Not only was I passed over for a desired promotion, the position they offered represented a considerable step backwards. Even if I uprooted my family and made the move, I did not know whether I would have a job after we completed the transition.

In the end, I swallowed my pride and took the job. I became more determined to prove myself; so long as I had some employment at General Mills, I still had the possibility to accomplish this goal. I knew I had the capability to do much more. After doing some research about Raleigh, Jeanette and I became excited about raising our family in this beautiful, gentile Southern city.

The move occurred in January 1970, and the ensuing months held for me some wonderful highs and difficult lows. My family became acclimated quickly, with our children settling into schools and a routine. We made friends, and started exploring North Carolina. The more moderate climate, even in January, certainly helped. Raleigh felt like home to us fairly quickly.

Professionally, it was another story which did not surprise me. It became evident pretty quickly that our division did not need two assistant controllers. We frequently duplicated efforts and, in effect, tripped over each other. I suspected yet again that my days with this division - and quite possibly General Mills - were numbered.

Still, weathering several suggestions that I *look for employment elsewhere* over the past few years actually accomplished something positive. With experience, I had grown stronger and smarter professionally. I actually became *more* confident in my abilities. The more others tried to diminish me, the more determined I became to prove them wrong. I started to view my professional setbacks as opportunities for growth, not indictments on my character or capabilities. I also learned that others' opinions of me mattered far less than my belief in myself.

Over and over again in life I have found that how I respond to difficult personal and professional situations matters far more than the situation itself. Dealing with career rejection only made me more confident to excel. Although I wanted to remain at General Mills, if needed, I had the confidence and experience now to move on.

Within several months, our controller moved to a different role at our company. Although I had the qualifications for and expressed an interest in the vacant position, the response came back clearly:

no. I again was strongly encouraged to seek employment elsewhere 'to better myself.'

In mid-1971, a new vice president of finance joined us from General Mills' headquarters in Minneapolis. Al Colling became a good friend and someone with whom I worked very well. He believed in my capabilities, and helped me get ready for the career advancement position I desired and worked hard to achieve. As a mentor, Al would prove invaluable.

It was our division president, not Al, who conducted my annual performance evaluation on that fateful day in 1972 when he dismissed my management abilities. After four years of working in this executive's organization, it became clear *to* me that changing his opinion *of* me may never occur.

That became a great lesson itself. Changing perceptions can take a long time, if it happens ever. Sometimes, personalities or styles simply clash or a leader may not like you. Trying to change others can become a losing proposition. Focusing energy and attention on becoming the most competent person *you* can be provides the greatest opportunity for long-term professional success. It was true during the 'gold watch' career days, and I believe it equally valid today.

With our fourth child, Jane, just a few months old, I decided to defer considering a job change. That proved to be a smart decision for my family and me. When Al returned to General Mills' headquarters, I finally got the promotion I sought and replaced him. Along with Al's support, perhaps I was rewarded for my loyalty and perseverance. Whatever contributed, the opportunity to prove myself in a true leadership role had arrived. My professional experiences instilled in me a strong determination to get it right.

I would not let myself, my family or my company down.

Chapter Four

ABOUT COURSE CORRECTION AND SEIZING OPPORTUNITY

"It may take several attempts before you can play the high notes on a clarinet, but never. ever give up until you get it right."

Hawkins Bradley and me, one month after acquiring GoodMark from General Foods, June 1982

It takes courage to push yourself to places you have never been before ... to test your limits .... author Anais Nin

I fondly recall high school as a time of many firsts in my life. I had my first girlfriend, owned my first car, had the first sense that I could have a life beyond farming, and began what has become a life-long enjoyment of music. At fifteen or sixteen years old, that musical interest led me to pick up a clarinet for the first time. Why the clarinet? Although I cannot remember exactly why I selected this instrument over, say, the snare drum or guitar, I do remember the enjoyment I received from trying to play it. Sadly, my talent lagged significantly behind my desire. Yet I remained committed to giving it my all.

My music instructor in school noticed my interest, and helped me develop my limited ability. I practiced hard to achieve my best. Over time I could play reasonably well and, the more proficient I became, the more challenging the pieces I selected to play.

With my music teacher's encouragement, I signed up for my first high school recital and ambitiously chose *Ave Maria* for my solo. I realized the challenge, but became determined to play it without error. I practiced over and over and over again to perfect the composition, paying particular attention to the hard-to-reach high upper C notes at its end.

The day of the recital came, and our main auditorium filled with hundreds of students and parents. Accompanied by a pianist (my music teacher), I began to play the piece. All went well until a loud, off-key squeak came out of my clarinet when I tried to reach the difficult high notes. You can imagine my horror and embarrassment, yet I tried playing again. The audience of my peers and their parents heard the squeak yet again. The sound that filled the auditorium was not my music, but laughter and some friendly heckling.

Some may have decided to stop playing or left the stage in failure, but I remember my determination to keep trying. I did not want to leave the stage in defeat. It would take several more attempts but by altering my approach just a little, I finally got it right and played the entire piece hitting all the notes! The audience stood, applauded and cheered - probably as much (if not more) for my tenacity and stubbornness. I happily left the stage a winner.

If at first you don't succeed, try, try again, would become a repetitive theme and my approach throughout my life, particularly when I felt passionate about something. My determination, tenacity and focus on *course correction* - seeking alternative solutions to accomplish a goal or solve a problem - began early. Mastering difficult-to-play notes represents just one of many examples. Over time, exercising those skills to accomplish would become second nature to me.

Becoming a problem solver early in life served me well. It helped me see that with hard work, a plan and flexibility to change that plan if needed, I could dream bigger than I ever imagined. Without it, for example, college and my business career likely would have been out-of-reach. I also found that nearly every success or accomplishment that had occurred in my life up until that point involved some level of risk. I grew to embrace taking chances as a necessary and important part of seizing opportunity and succeeding. I wanted to be fearless.

When October 13, 1981 started, I had no idea how a corporate decision - and putting those well-developed skills to the test - would change the trajectory of my career and life.

Although the timing of General Mills' announcement that it intended to sell GoodMark surprised many including me, corporate decisions made years earlier seemed destined to seal the fate of our division.

The creation of GoodMark in 1970 from the combination of the Garner, North Carolina-based Jesse Jones Sausage Co. and Adolph Levis' company which became Slim Jim, Inc. initially held great promise for success and profitability. It aligned with General Mills' corporate strategy during the late 1960's and 1970's to diversify its portfolio of food product offerings beyond their well-known, mainstream brands. Who does not know Betty Crocker, Wheaties, Cheerios and Gold Medal flour? In creating a new Consumer Specialties Division, they hoped over time to create brand recognition for other products leading to corporate growth and profitability.

Overall, our company did well for several years. I also did well, and thrived in a leadership role that I had worked hard to earn. I felt that my years of career lows finally had paid off. I had stayed true to my values, and through hard work had earned the respect of General Mills' senior management. I perceived I had an upward career trajectory with the company. Professionally, life was good.

As the 1970's ended, two unmistakable signs of trouble began brewing for GoodMark. First, decisions were made to change the *Slim Jim* formula and increase the per item selling price. My strong and vocal opposition to this strategy fell on deaf ears. I felt we insulted our loyal customers by asking them to pay more for a product that I thought had less quality.

Not surprising to me, sales and profits began suffering.

Next, General Mills strategically decided to streamline its diversified product strategy and focus on its core products. It certainly did not take a rocket scientist to see the writing on the wall.

Unless changes occurred quickly, I felt our division was in big trouble. As I had several times over my twenty year career at General Mills, I found myself wondering about my professional future. More immediately, I became very concerned about GoodMark's future and what would happen to our loyal and hardworking team.

General Mills would not keep the formal announcement of their intentions quiet for long. I remember the events of October 13, 1981 like they happened yesterday. That day, I learned from my bosses during a meeting at the Howard Johnson's hotel on Capital Boulevard in Raleigh, North Carolina about General Mills' decision to divest GoodMark from their corporate portfolio.

I had hoped for a different result. While not always a vacation, I thrived at GoodMark after our move from Philadelphia to Raleigh. I had terrific colleagues. I enjoyed a fantastic home life with Jeanette and our growing family of four children, not to mention a great circle of friends. I also had achieved a measure of professional stability for the first time in my career at General Mills. That was about to change.

My leadership not only broke the news to me that fateful October day, they strongly encouraged me to begin a job search as soon as possible. I must admit, I had a strong sense of déjà vu given the number of times that piece of advice had come my way throughout my General Mills' tenure.

What did intrigue me during that meeting? I learned that General Mills did not have a buyer yet. Did this potentially present an opportunity for me to fulfill my dream of owning a business?

My bosses may have thought that I would take their advice about beginning my job search immediately. That was a reasonable assumption.

Jeanette and I recently made a down payment to move our family into a much larger home, and college tuition for our four children required significant financial planning. I faced increased household expenses just as my job security became more precarious. During the meeting, my thoughts turned to my career prospects. Could I get another job within General Mills? What challenges would I have as a 46-year old seasoned professional even finding employment outside of the only company I had faithfully worked at for twenty years?

Our leadership probably thought that like any GoodMark employee hearing this news, I left the meeting fearful, uncertain and concerned.

I actually felt strangely *excited*. Over the years since the shopping mall disappointment, I had dreamed of owning a business. I even had passing thoughts years ago about buying the Jesse Jones Sausage Company from General Mills. I had fourteen years of experience with this division, and knew the business potential well.

Privately, I wondered whether General Mills could get a buyer for our struggling division. Could I help return this once-successful company to profitability? Did General Mills' decision present an once-in-a-lifetime opportunity for me to buy the company?

Long ago, I heard the following about risk: *the greater the challenge, the riskier the move, the sweeter the reward.* It stuck with me.

As I did so many times throughout my life, I could not wait to get home and discuss my career options with my most trusted advisor. That evening, Jeanette listened as I recounted the day's events culminating with the strong potential that my days as a General Mills' employee had become numbered. With our significant and mounting financial responsibilities and four children, she naturally felt some legitimate concern. Yet, I also remember the broad smile on her face and the gleam in her eye when I told her that General Mills' unexpected decision presented a chance of a lifetime for me to possibly make my long-standing dream of owning a business a reality.

This unexpected course correction caused me to completely shift my professional priorities in a direction that I could not have imagined even twenty-four hours prior. With Jeanette's support, I vowed to do everything in my power to evaluate the legitimacy of buying GoodMark. If successful, I would have a chance to own a business that I felt confident I could lead successfully. If I failed, I would have no regrets that I allowed this opportunity to pass me by without trying. I could see no downside from at least exploring the potential.

That very evening, I began working on a plan of action. I also called Hawkins Bradley, GoodMark's Vice President of Operations and the former co-owner of Jesse Jones Sausage Company.

Hawkins and I had worked side-by-side together at GoodMark for many years. We enjoyed a similar business philosophy, and became good friends.

I trusted him completely.

Hawkins listened intently as I told him my idea of putting together a management buy-out proposal to purchase GoodMark from General Mills. I thought it a step in the right direction that I had his attention and the prospect intrigued him. He neither laughed nor suggested that I needed psychiatric help, both positive results from my perspective! We agreed to keep our conversation confidential until I could work up numbers for a legitimate purchase price and cash flow statement.

I hung up the telephone very excited. If my wife and my trusted business associate saw potential, perhaps we had a chance.

I immediately took action. Adrenaline and large quantities of caffeine fueled my all-nighter on October 13th when I began to develop the financial and strategic proposals we would need to encourage General Mills to take our offer and us seriously. As I worked through initial estimates of a purchase price and Statement of Cash Flow, it became clear that no matter how we structured the deal we would have to borrow a large amount of money to make the purchase a reality.

With interest rates at 18-20% during this time, I remained excited yet very aware of the significant financial risk my family would assume by acquiring this company. Throughout the many weeks of developing the deal, I would ask myself several times whether the potential reward of owning my own company outweighed the financial risk that could negatively impact my family and our financial future.

Opportunities to fulfill your dreams do not come along every day, and I remained committed to putting together the best deal I could before deciding whether to move forward. A few days later, I had developed a working business plan and, with the addition of our colleagues and new partners Don Axberg and David Loge, a viable management team critical to qualifying with General Mills' requirements for the sale.

I remember my excitement when I invited Hawkins, Don and David to our first official planning meeting at Hawkins' home a few days after learning about General Mills' intention to sell. One of our first orders of business involved establishing the new company's officers. Based on the experience and expertise each of us brought to the table, we unanimously agreed to appoint Hawkins as president with Don, David and me serving as vice presidents. We also began refining the cash flow and income statements that we ultimately used to buy GoodMark.

In the weeks between mid-October and Thanksgiving, by day, we performed our jobs at General Mills. At night and on weekends, Hawkins,

Don, David and I worked with little sleep to confidentially put together all of the necessary puzzle pieces to make a proposal to General Mills legitimate. We knew that we had to act fast before General Mills found another potential buyer. With my accounting and financial expertise, it fell primarily to me to talk with numerous bankers and accountants during this period with a goal of putting together the necessary financing to make our management buy-out proposal credible. One thing I knew for sure: making this deal work would require the confidence of bankers in our leadership team's ability to make this business profitable.

Most of my efforts during this intense period focused on working with law firms, accountants and other financial professionals confidentially to determine the financial package that would persuade General Mills to sell to our team. Based on business valuation and other factors, the magic number that our experts thought would get General Mills' attention approximated $31 million. One big problem existed. Through savings, high interest rate loans and other financing, my partners and I still could not come to closing with anything near that much cash. General Mills strong desire to sell and no other buyers on the horizon worked in our favor. We decided to get creative.

The unique and complex proposal that we developed for General Mills' consideration was an early example of what became known in the business world as a 'leveraged buy-out.' Our offered purchase price of just over $31 million would include a small amount of cash up front (about $200,000), with the remainder coming from a combination of debt and royalties. The debt included bank loans and a small revolving line of credit from General Mills that we would pay back with interest.

The proposal provided a win-win for all parties concerned. General Mills could divest itself of the company and still benefit financially from our success through royalties and debt interest payments. Our management team could purchase the company and, from my perspective, successfully run a business.

Shortly after Thanksgiving 1981, we had completed the necessary steps to make General Mills a legitimate offer. Our team had many hurdles to overcome before an actual purchase might occur, but we had made progress in a very short period of time! Over thirty years later, I still remember my excitement.

Our first opportunity to publicly announce our intention to buy GoodMark came just after New Year's Day in January 1982 when our company president returned from his holiday vacation. I vividly recall arranging a meeting with him on his first day back to discuss an urgent matter to include Hawkins, Don, David and me. I opened the meeting by informing him that we had assembled an offer to buy GoodMark from General Mills. The shocked look on his face told me that we surprised him. He immediately called General Mills in our presence to advise them of our intentions, and posted a bulletin in our office announcing our plan to employees. I fully anticipated that we might lose our jobs that day, but he allowed us to stay. To this day I do not know why, and suspect he thought General Mills would decline our offer. Many did not take us seriously. Perhaps he fell in that camp too.

After four long months of discussions and negotiations with General Mills, we did succeed! On May 26, 1982, our team closed on the purchase of GoodMark for $31.5 million, with the official date of ownership transfer occurring on May 30th. Our tenacity, creativity, desire and some good luck paid off. This moment ranks as one of the most exciting of my professional career. Despite long odds, we persevered and accomplished our goal. I enjoyed wonderful celebrations with family and friends, and excitedly looked forward to the next chapter in my professional life.

I could not wait to let our talented employees know about our vision which included them as a big part of our success plan.

Shortly after we closed, I called a meeting with Hawkins, Don and David so that we could discuss the agenda for our meeting with employees. I anticipated a big celebration and the beginning of a new chapter for GoodMark.

I had no idea that I would face another professional course correction and potential setback so soon.

My euphoria at having just accomplished my professional goal quickly turned to disappointment and frustration during that meeting. All three of my partners informed me that they had no interest in growing the business; they wanted to sell the company for what they hoped would be a quick profit!

Blindsided, stunned and angry describe what I felt at that moment. I sincerely thought that we all shared the same vision to build a successful business. Clearly, I was mistaken.

I faced yet another situation in my career where I played the clarinet and struggled to reach the high note. Do I keep trying until I succeed or should I get off the stage and acknowledge defeat?

Since my first entrepreneurial experience many years earlier, I had dreamed of owning a business again. I had no intention of getting off the stage. I did not want to sell the company for a quick profit. I believed in the economic potential of our products and wanted to see the business grow. I anticipated potential future challenges from sales, market share, changing demographics and other variables - but was excited about tackling them. I wanted to provide the loyal and hardworking GoodMark employees with opportunities, and to see how far we could take the company.

Thankfully, after talking with Hawkins he stayed. As our current cash position did not allow us to buy out the other two partners immediately, we agreed to pay each $2.25 million, paid out over three years.

The experience of purchasing GoodMark taught me many important lessons that apply to business and life, including:

- Seize an opportunity when it presents itself! You never know when you may have it again, if ever. I often said 'he who hesitates, loses.'
- Have business partners who share your vision. Clearly communicate your goals and listen carefully to what you hear from them in return.
- Do not allow your excitement to override common sense or good business judgment.
- Expect the unexpected, and prepare contingency plans. The ability to correct your course when needed can make the difference between success and failure.
- Believe in your abilities even when others may not.
- Not everyone can stomach significant financial or other risk. Honestly evaluate the potential risk against the reward, and make a decision right for your family and you.
- Stay true to your ethics and values.

- Ask yourself *if I do not move forward, will I regret it?* Make decisions in your career (and life) to avoid 'what ifs.' Learn from your mistakes and apply those lessons to future decisions.
- Enjoy not just the destination, but the process of getting there.
- Have fun!

From May 26, 1982 when we succeeded in purchasing GoodMark from General Mills until my retirement in July 1999 (after we sold the business to ConAgra in 1998), I would find myself having to play the clarinet over and over again to hit those high notes.

I never once regretted staying on the stage.

My license plate for nearly thirty years - and still on my car today.

The reverse side of my Official Retirement Autograph Card, prepared by our Marketing Department as a surprise for me, 1999. Celebrating my dual roles as CEO and 'Macho Man' Doggett!

Chapter Five

ABOUT LEADERSHIP

*"Real leaders inspire those around them
to become their very best."*

GoodMark Board of Directors, 1987

I briefly have met General Colin Powell on a few occasions, and found him impressive and inspiring. This includes in 1997 when, during my tenure serving on the WakeMed Foundation board of directors, he spoke at a recognition event for our non-profit's supporters. General Powell is credited with saying *"great leaders are almost always great simplifiers, who can cut through argument, debate, and doubt to offer a solution everybody can understand."* I could not agree more. Real leaders possess a gift for bringing people with different perspectives, personalities and talents together.

Spend some time reviewing the *Management* shelves of any bookstore. Literally hundreds of books exist which promote the virtues of different leadership styles.

In my humble opinion, we make leadership more complicated than necessary. My experience with executives in farming (that is, my dad), the military, business, universities and non-profits has taught me that leaders basically fall into one of two camps.

The *Camp A* leader encourages the best from direct reports and the people around him or her. He leads by example and creates a motivating work environment. Transparency; good communication; and individual accomplishment and accountability are all non-negotiable expectations. This visionary participates as part of a team, not above it. Like a successful sports team coach, this leader *inspires* his players resulting in individual and team accomplishment. Clearly communicating goals, helping individuals achieve their highest potential and recognizing contributions makes for a satisfied, enthusiastic and motivated work force. If each spoke on the team wheel functions in a productive manner, it allows the wheel to turn.

We all likely have had experiences with the *Camp B* leader who cares more about his self-promotion than the people around him. This manager makes decisions that positively impact him with limited or no regard for individuals on the team. He generally takes credit for most team ideas and successes. He commands neither respect nor loyalty. Direct reports do not trust him, and generally with good reason. These managers have teams with higher turnover, lower morale, increased conflict and less productivity. Who wants to work long-term for someone who neither respects individual contribution nor acts with integrity?

Throughout my life, I have had the good fortune to work for leaders in both camps. I say 'good fortune' because I learned as much if not more from executives that undervalued my capabilities or disrespected me. Much can be learned from a supervisor who behaves like a dictator, bully or CIA spy harboring state secrets.

My dad provided me with my earliest example of the kind of leader I hoped to become.

He set clear expectations for performance. I trusted him. I knew he had as his top priority the best interests of our family. He kept his word. He knew how to delegate and communicated clearly my area of responsibility and accountabilities on the farm and to our family. He led by example. Although not effusive with praise, his 'good job' truly meant something.

He motivated me to give 120% effort to my tasks every day.

One might think that the command and control nature of the military encourages a *one size fits all* leadership style. My Army experience taught me that nothing could be further from the truth. I had the maturing experience of working with officers in both camps of leadership, and found that management ability and approach in the military mirrors that of other organizations.

While stationed at Fort Bliss, Texas, I reported to a Master Sargent who I quickly grew to admire and respect. He could not have been a better boss. With his boss, the Commandant, together they had over sixty years of military experience; over their many years, they had seen just about everything a military leader can see.

During my military tenure, I observed them closely as they dealt with serious allegations, behavioral problems and crimes including AWOL (absent without leave), poor performance, marital issues, insubordination, stealing, substance abuse and the list goes on.

They impressed and amazed me with the methodical, unemotional and fair way they handled each situation. They applied their expectations for conduct and performance equally among all, and I did not once see them show favoritism or bias. They thoroughly investigated each situation. They took the time necessary to evaluate, conclude and execute. Consistency, intelligence, predictability, calmness and follow thorough describe both men. They held soldiers accountable for their actions, with punishments that matched the severity of the infraction. Their words and tone inspired respect and confidence.

They exemplified great leadership every day, not just when problems arose. Both men knew how to motivate and get results. They communicated expectations clearly, and demanded excellence from themselves and us. I proudly served with and for them. I hoped to have the opportunity to emulate their leadership style one day.

During my first twenty years at General Mills, I became a student of leadership in the work place. What an extraordinary class! I did not have to pay tuition, yet gained tremendous experience that would pay me future dividends and rewards. I paid attention to the actions, demeanor, words and non-verbal behaviors of bosses in both camps, and planned for the type of leader I wanted to become when my opportunity arrived.

I also took responsibility to learn more about leadership than my job could teach me. I studied the careers of company CEO's who I admired, some of whom I worked with through serving on their boards of directors. I got to know the executives with whom I attended Harvard's Advanced Management Program and stayed in contact with several after its completion. I joined leadership and professional organizations including the National Association of Corporate Directors (NACD), and networked with many talented professionals also affiliated with these groups. In my philanthropic activities I worked closely with, and observed the leadership styles of, executives at universities and several non-profits.

I readily acknowledged that I did not know it all. Far from it. I asked questions of other managers that I respected.

I *listened* to their answers.

I remain a student of leadership to this day. Motivating individuals and teams to become their very best continues to excite me.

So what has over a half century of experience taught me about directing others? Some of the most important lessons learned by me early in my life and career remain equally valid today. When I finally got my opportunity to lead, I made it my mission to incorporate these outstanding principles into creating an inspired culture. I now could treat the talented people of GoodMark as I had wanted to be treated. I certainly made mistakes along the way - and learned from them too.

Lesson #1:

Do Not Give a Marketing Job to an Accountant.

Throughout my career, I witnessed several instances where a mismatch existed between an employee's skills and the job's requirements. Over the years, I worked for a few of those people.

Did responsibility for the lack of success fall on the leader who made the hire or the employee who accepted a position that did not align with his experience, skills and background? Perhaps both have some blame. I clearly remember the disruptive impact - resulting in lost momentum, frustration, lower productivity and decreased morale.

Today, we call aligning position needs with employee capabilities *hiring smart*. Everyone has talents. A good leader knows the style, skills, capabilities, and experience required for every role on his team and hires accordingly. This establishes the critical foundation for both individual and team success. Teams pay an unfortunate price when unnecessary turnover occurs, and good leaders minimize it at all costs by doing their best to hire right the first time.

Lesson #2:

If You Say Something, Do It.

Great leaders inspire because their actions support their words. This in turn builds trust and respect. When long hours were required to build our company, employees saw me lead by example and work eighty+ hours a week. If I made an employee a promise, I kept it or communicated why circumstances had changed. I expected this conduct from my leadership team as well.

Building trust with employees takes repeated and consistent positive experiences and can erode with just one broken promise.

Lesson #3:

Straight Shooters Hit the Bulls Eye Every Time.

What does *good communication* really mean?

At GoodMark, we enjoyed success and made mistakes. As discussed in this book, I authorized buying a struggling, cash poor trail mix company; a start-up refrigerated brownie company and a competing meat snack company. For a variety of reasons, these acquisitions did not succeed. We could have divested them quietly.

However, I felt it very important to explain to our employees why we made the purchase decisions; why the acquisitions did not serve the company's best interest; what we learned from the failures; and what we planned to do going forward.

Treating employees like adults with respect and clearly communicating progress toward team goals, organizational successes, developments - and mistakes - has numerous rewards and benefits. It encourages a workforce's investment in and commitment to an organization's achievement. It also helps to minimize rumors which can erode morale. Telling our troops the truth in good and bad times became an important part of my leadership and communication style.

Employees also became accustomed to seeing me frequently. I made it a point to walk around our offices and plants to both listen to and talk with them one-on-one. I got to know them as individuals and they, in turn, got to know me. They saw by my actions that I cared. I asked them for their input and gave them credit when we implemented one of their ideas.

As our company got larger and more successful, I informally met with employees in small groups. I made it a priority to listen to them and create an environment where they could provide honest, open feedback. We also had more formal, expertise-specific committees like Marketing, Quality Control, and Research and Development comprised of our employees who knew these areas best. These sessions produced many benefits like relationship development and collegiality - and some great ideas resulted.

I always have felt that when problem-solving, two minds (or more) generally come up with better ideas than one.

To me, good communication occurs when employees feel leadership *hears* them and when they receive information about the organization in a clear, concise and honest way.

It was a culture that we worked hard to create.

Lesson #4:

Have 20-20 Vision.

What do we believe in and stand for as an organization? How can our employees contribute to achieving our company's short- and long-range goals? Have circumstances changed which require us to adapt our vision or goals? These questions consumed a lot of my time as chief executive.

Clear vision comes from leadership determining the direction and pathway for an organization's success. A leader, like a general in battle, has a blueprint for how to take an organization from Point A to Point B. Good leaders can develop a clear plan that tells everyone what to expect, sell it and encourage others to excitedly join them on the journey to execute it. What happens then? Buy-in results.

When circumstances change, plans also need to change. An effective leader can recognize when to course correct, and help others adapt.

We used a variety of methods to keep employees apprised of our blueprint – and blueprint changes. Team meetings became a very effective forum. Not only would our leaders communicate with our workforce, but employees were encouraged to ask questions and communicate back. This open dialogue enhanced employee understanding, thereby contributing to successful implementation of the new expectations or goals.

No matter how effectively a leader communicates, not all decisions will be understood, liked or supported. Yet, treating your workforce with respect and making them a valued part of the process will help to encourage their understanding, if not their complete agreement.

Lesson #5:

Hire Smart. *Really* Smart.

I could never understand managers who feel threatened by, or competitive with, the smart people who work for and with them.

Over the years, the leaders I most admired exuded confidence in themselves and their teams. They recognized their strengths - and improvement areas. They understood that they singularly could not make the organization successful. It takes a team of people with different experiences, skills, personality traits and interests. They surrounded themselves with highly capable talent who compensated for the skills they lacked. They delegated, and gave ownership and accountability for success to others.

Delegation would prove to be a challenge for me in my early months of leading GoodMark. While I hired gifted managers, I foolishly and incorrectly thought that for employees to respect me I had to know and become involved with virtually all aspects of running the company. I quickly learned that this would not become a long-term formula for success or effectiveness. I began to frustrate the talented people in marketing, sales and other critical functions around me who had the skills I lacked and did not have the empowerment to effectively do their jobs.

I needed to adapt my leadership style - and fast.

Micro-managing benefits absolutely no one, and leads to demoralized employees. Fortunately, I learned pretty quickly that delegation gives talent the responsibility, ownership and accountability to accomplish. Great things happened! This also had the added benefit of allowing me to focus on the areas of responsibility that I, as chief executive, could - and should - most impact.

Lesson #6:

Surround Yourself With People Who Share Your Core Values.

Over the years, I have met visionary leaders who differ in style, personality and approach. However, they shared a well-developed set of personal values including ethics, morality, honesty, trustworthiness, fairness, professionalism and integrity.

Smart and successful leaders set an example of how they expect their employees to behave in the work place by how they act. *Do as I say and not as I do* does not work when raising children – and it certainly does not work at work either!

My direct reports clearly understood my expectations of employee treatment and integrity in our work place. My executive team had different strengths, experiences and personalities which made the group strong; in ethics, I expected uniformity.

At times, managers with strong technical skills did not succeed at our company because their personal values and leadership style simply did not align with our expectations.

Lesson #7:

The Buck Stops with the Leader.

President Harry Truman got it right.

When I made mistakes, and I made plenty, I took responsibility for them - and for fixing them. I expected the same from my management team. With leadership comes responsibility; a leader who tried to offload blame onto an employee quickly would lose my respect - and quite possibly their job.

Employees want to know that their leadership supports them. When those in charge take personal responsibility, it helps to create staff loyalty, trust and respect.

Lesson #8:

Work to Retain Talent.

Working to create an enviable culture and professional opportunities to retain our talent would become one of my top priorities throughout my tenure at GoodMark. Why?

I firmly believe that a company's best resource, no matter its product or service, is its *people*. Generally, an organization spends significant time and money to train a new employee so that he (or she) begins with the right foundation for success. This investment can produce great returns for both the individual and the organization. High turnover can signify big trouble. Not only can it hurt productivity and morale, it also is very costly. Creating a culture and working environment that encourages retention can produce significant benefits including to the organization's bottom line.

Our GoodMark executive team worked hard to create an environment that would encourage our talent to build a career with us. Culture can be a difficult concept to quantify. Why do people thrive in some organizations and fail in others?

So how did we try and encourage loyalty?

- Implementation of competitive pay, bonus and benefits plans with compensation tied to performance. This helped put everyone on an even playing field and created incentives to excel.
- The company's success became our employees' success. Use of stock options, for example, to reward proved highly motivating.
- We actively tried to promote from within as much as possible. This motivated our loyal employees and

gave them faith that their hard work could provide opportunity.

- Recognition to applaud individual and team successes and milestones occurred regularly. As an example, we recognized accomplishment in key performance areas like safety, cost reduction and sales growth.

- Hosting events to include employee spouses and families occurred throughout the year. In addition to an annual holiday party, we had picnics, bowling teams and other occasions to encourage relationship development and collegiality.

- We sponsored college scholarships for children of company staff, with ceremonies attended by GoodMark employees to congratulate the awardees and their families.

- A newsletter both informed and recognized our employees. I wrote a personal column to highlight key corporate developments and, most importantly, thank them for their efforts and hard work.

- We encouraged employee ideas and feedback; when we implemented a suggestion, we gave recognition to the employee with the great idea.

- Public recognition of employees for a job well done, promotion or other success as well as welcoming new staff occurred without fail.
- Treating our employees like family to include a member of leadership, including me, attending funerals, weddings and other special events occurred whenever possible. This became more challenging as the company grew, but we did our best; hopefully our colleagues knew it.

I learned that motivating employees with a handshake, smile, warm hello, hug, congratulations or thank you takes such little effort, yet can pay big dividends in job satisfaction and retention. Adherence to *The Golden Rule* became an expectation.

Lesson #9:

Encourage a Culture of Diverse Opinions, Not Rubber Stamping.

At GoodMark, some of the best ideas we implemented to solve serious business problems came from energized, spirited and sometimes passionate debates. By hiring smart and encouraging our talent to speak up, solutions brought forward delighted me.

Frequently others - not me - presented the best ideas and the ones we eventually implemented. Talk about boosting morale!

I believe that strong leaders encourage a free expression of approaches and ideas. Companies where only the boss can have the good or implemented suggestions, are places where talent stays for only a short time.

Of course, once we made a decision, we expected all to support it. Yet allowing for input encouraged that buy-in.

Lesson #10:

Have *Passion*

I saved the best for last.

I sometimes am asked why and how I persevered at General Mills and GoodMark during times of significant trials, tribulations and disappointments. Why did I not move on to greener pastures, so to speak, when encouraged by leadership at General Mills to find another job?

I always answer with one word - *passion*. I truly loved our business, my colleagues and our customers. I came to work most days energized by the opportunity to make a difference at our company.

Leaders who convey this excitement have the greatest opportunity for success. If you believe that you can succeed and you feel it in your belly every day, it's a good bet that you will persevere and come out on top.

If *you* think it, believe it and expect it, chances are your employees will too.

Chapter Six

ABOUT INTEGRITY

*"Integrity matters in **every** situation."*

My children, Jane, Michael, Anne and Mark.
They define 'integrity.'

One of the darkest chapters of my career occurred just after our successful acquisition of GoodMark from General Mills in May 1982.

The first few months of owning the company would prove unexpectedly eventful with a roller coaster ride of emotions. Elation quickly turned into panic when all three of my partners announced they wanted to sell, followed by excitement when Hawkins agreed to stay, culminating in relief when we negotiated a settlement to buy out our two partners. I thought we had overcome all of the post-acquisition hiccups.

I finally could look forward to running the company.

Not so fast.

About eight weeks after buying the business, I received an unexpected phone call from a General Mills' attorney. Getting right to the point, he told me that General Mills determined a calculation error occurred at closing and we owed them over $2 million in additional compensation.

For a minute, I thought very funny the practical joke that the as-yet unknown prankster and I would chuckle about for many years to come.

When I realized this was no joke, I wasted no time to strenuously object. I reminded him that we followed the closing guidelines - developed by General Mills - to the letter. I asked for specifics as to how they determined a cash shortfall occurred, and strongly disagreed with the complex, multipart explanation provided. A business dispute between us ensued.

I hung up the phone in shock. As a loyal General Mills employee for over twenty years, I deeply respected the company and my colleagues there. Purchasing GoodMark represented a win-win for both General Mills and me. After many months of trying to sell the business, the only legitimate offer General Mills received to buy it as far as I knew came from our team. They sold a division they no longer wanted, and I fulfilled my career dream. I anticipated maintaining a strong relationship with the company. The dispute put that in jeopardy. On a personal level, I did not want my relationship with General Mills to become adversarial. I still thought of them as family.

After our lengthy and exhaustive efforts to purchase GoodMark, another unexpected obstacle threatened us. General Mills just went through the closing with us, so they must have known that we neither had the millions demanded nor the cash resources to fight. I quickly became concerned that *we could potentially lose the business*. Whether I agreed or not, we did not have the deeper pockets.

General Mills requested that we allow their auditors to review our financial records. This also surprised me. We had been completely transparent throughout the closing process. I wondered what I should infer from this demand. Perhaps, they did not trust us. Could it be possible, for example, that they perceived we intentionally devalued our business to reduce the purchase price making their demands for more money legitimate? Did they think we withheld information? We bought one of their companies, and they had access to the same information we had before closing. What did they think they would find by auditing us *after the sale*?

Disputing some of the specifics in a business transaction is one thing. I now felt that my integrity and ethics were being called into question. This made me absolutely livid. I am not a thief.

I had mixed feelings about allowing an audit. While it most certainly would vindicate us, we had just bought the business and I wanted our team to focus on running and growing it. To move forward, not spend time looking back. An audit, particularly if it lasted many days or weeks, could create an unnecessary distraction from what we needed to accomplish. I did not want to lose momentum.

However, after careful consideration and assessing the pros and cons with our attorneys, I agreed. The sooner we could get this behind us, the better.

The audit lasted several days and involved an exhaustive review of our finances and record keeping. I had complete confidence that the auditors would find everything in order. *When you make decisions and operate with principles, ethics and integrity as your first priority, you have nothing to worry about.*

When the auditors issued their written report validating our processes and confirming that they found no mistakes or irregular activities, I felt elated and vindicated. We had proven our case, and General Mills and our team could go back to running our respective businesses.

I thought it was over.

It was not. Despite their auditors' findings, they still believed we owed them money. They went forward with a lawsuit, a dark day for me. After coming so far, I did not intend to lose the business now. Although I believed we could prevail, I feared that we might win the battle but lose the proverbial war. Our attorneys agreed. We could spend precious time, money and resources fighting, or we could settle the dispute quickly and move on.

I felt more comfortable compromising over money now that I had fought and won to preserve a much more important commodity: *my integrity.*

I learned a valuable lesson. Lose money, and you can rebuild. Lose your reputation, and it may take a lifetime to reestablish it - if you ever can. I also learned that picking your battles wisely matters. We negotiated a settlement, and put our energy and time into running the company instead of a protracted fight.

I think we made the right decision. GoodMark's success over the next sixteen years speaks for itself. I also resumed my relationships with several of my General Mills colleagues once the dispute 'dust' settled. This made me very happy.

Throughout my career, I made thousands of decisions. I took lots of risks, sometimes big ones, but always after careful thought and consideration. Sometimes, they worked out even better than I anticipated. The purchase of GoodMark illustrates this. When the opportunity presented itself, I wanted to do everything possible, leave no stone unturned, to see if we actually could acquire the company. Making it happen was the thrill of a lifetime.

Sometimes my decisions led to results that did not work out. I could write a whole book on my mistakes and what I learned. A few notable (and also mentioned elsewhere in this book) ill-advised decisions stand out.

A few years after acquiring the business, we had an opportunity to diversify our product lines by buying a cash poor trail mix business and a cashless, start up, baked goods company. While both companies had good products, acquiring them diverted our attention and resources from our highly profitable meat snack business - our expertise. What did we know about trail mix or brownies?

Ironically, it was General Mills' desire to divest of its specialty product lines and return to its 'core' products that created the opportunity for me to acquire GoodMark in the first place! I should have known better. I learned quickly to stick with what you know and do it well.

Divesting of these companies happened fairly quickly, and I applied the valuable lessons learned to future decisions.

To quickly grow market share and increase distribution, I authorized the acquisition of a competing meat snack company. Based on the research and our strategic plan, I believed that we could grow our business faster through this purchase. This proved completely wrong for our business! I learned that you actually can dilute your own well-respected brands by acquiring products perceived by your customers as inferior. When you have well-known products with a large percentage of market share and a competitor on the run, investing in your own products and company can prove more successful than acquiring a failing business.

However, whether successful or ill-advised, any decision I made had to meet the 'right/wrong' test. If a decision did not align with my values, morals or integrity, I simply did not do it. I honestly can say that in a career spanning nearly forty years, I never made a business decision that compromised my ethics. *Ever.*

Over the years, I tried to surround myself professionally with people who share my values.

I also sought to surround myself with diversity - people with different backgrounds, religions, political persuasions, religious affiliations and experiences - and hired accordingly. I wanted and expected people to challenge me. But, I remained unwavering that they needed a well-defined sense of right and wrong. I conducted myself with transparency and the highest values and morals, and expected those with whom I worked to do the same.

I tried to be a good example for them - and my children.

I also went to great lengths to avoid any appearance of impropriety. In Raleigh, North Carolina, we enjoy a small and close-knit business community. Business relationships frequently turn into friendships. From time-to-time, our leadership team wanted to select a business consultant or partner with whom I had a personal connection. Many of these potential contracts and relationships involved the exchange of substantial sums of money.

In those instances, I removed myself from the contract negotiating process and had one of my direct reports or another manager oversee the business relationship. I applied a conservative test to determine my participation. Sometimes, I could have stayed involved with no appearance of impropriety. I let my conscience guide me to make my best decisions. It never disappointed me.

Throughout my life, I often have said *I am what I am*. What you see is what you get. You cannot make everyone happy. Some people simply may not like you. You *can* stay true to your principles, and I always tried to do just that. The same principles I learned by working side-by-side with my dad on our family farm guided me in my professional and personal decision making.

I heard my dad's voice in my head many times during my tenure at GoodMark. I hope I made him proud.

Chapter Seven

ABOUT MISTAKES, SETBACKS AND FAILURES

"There is no such thing as failure.
Some outcomes just work better than others."

My son Michael and me in front of Slim Jim #44.
Many career and company ups and downs occurred
on the 'road' to success.

At times, the English language can confuse. It has nuance. It can create misunderstandings. Words or phrases frequently mean different things to different people, and they can evoke a variety of emotions. Interesting debates and discussions in politics, law, economics and religion occur over interpretations of what words mean. Hundreds, if not thousands, of books extoll the virtues of *good communication*. Motivating or demotivating your direct reports, colleagues or children can occur simply through the words you select and how you say them. Communicating well often can involve more art than science.

Yet, utter some words or phrases and you likely will get a universally similar interpretation of the meaning and intent. Although I have no concrete evidence to support this, I feel comfortable saying that hearing the words *you're fired* or *you should look for another job* generally will evoke a negative reaction in most people. I certainly felt that way many times when I thought my career at General Mills had ended.

Failure has the power to evoke a similar universal reaction. *Failure = bad. Failure = loser.* Successful people do not *fail*. When an end result does not go as expected or desired, it frequently leads to the question 'what went wrong?' or 'what's wrong with me?' as though we only had one potential outcome. Entrepreneurs, however, know better. *Failure* can simply lead us to a much better fit; a more profitable or desired path; less stressful personal and professional partnerships; or just a plain better result.

My book collaborator recently mentioned that she heard that successful author J.K. Rowling received *twelve* rejections before succeeding on her thirteenth attempt to publish her first *Harry Potter* book. Twelve 'no's' represents a setback by any standard, yet the author clearly stayed determined to have her manuscript published. It took some time, but it seems that she developed a business relationship with a partner who appreciated her vision. The rest is history.

The airplane, automobile and virtually all modern conveniences we take for granted today took many, many tries. Many of the failed attempts provided the inventors with knowledge previously unknown leading to the successful outcome they desired. In life and business, sometimes events occur which can change how we define success. A smart person recognizes those opportunities and alters course.

Say someone interviews for a job he (or she) thinks he wants and does not receive the job offer. After the initial disappointment fades, the person has a choice. He can view himself negatively as a failure since he did not achieve the desired end result. Or, he can learn from the experience; develop relationships with the new contacts he now has; perhaps take classes to enhance or learn new skills; and apply this knowledge at the next interview. This just may produce a more desired result despite the initial setback.

I believe that in most instances, failure as we generally define it does not exist; *some results work better than others.* Failing can be necessary and liberating on the road to success. Failure is not the opposite of success; *it leads us to success.* Cutting our losses and moving on to something else that will produce a better result saves an enormous amount of time, money and heartache.

As I have explained in this book, throughout my life, learning from my disappointments actually has served me well. My professional mistakes, beginning with my ill-advised attempt to develop a shopping mall during my college years to my frustrations during my General Mills' career, made me even more determined to learn and move forward. The disappointment and frustration I felt when passed over for promotions, after accepting my first GoodMark opportunity in Philadelphia, or receiving the *you are not management material* performance evaluation eventually gave way to my desire to prove myself at all costs.

My determination started early and has stayed with me throughout my life. I used setbacks to learn, gain skills and double my efforts to prepare myself. I believed in myself even when others did not. If I really wanted something, I rarely waved the white flag in defeat. Losing the occasional battle only made me more determined to ultimately win the war of achieving my career and life goals.

The path which led me to the management buy-out of GoodMark was littered with many mistakes and disappointments. Yet over the years I sometimes wondered, and discussed with Jeanette many times, whether I would have had such a strong determination to buy GoodMark if my General Mills' career had been smooth sailing. Although hard to know for sure, it certainly made for some interesting conversations with my wife over several glasses of good wine!

As this book documents, the setbacks did not magically end after we acquired the company. Far from it! From day one, when all three of my partners shocked me by announcing their desire to sell the business and cash out, time and time again I would face obstacles that would force me to either dig deep and find a solution or give up.

At times, admittedly, some of the obstacles tested my faith and caused more than an occasional sleepless night.

The post-closing disagreement with General Mills exemplifies one of those occasions. I could have lost the business, not to mention my dream. It also represents one of my proudest moments. Whether intended or not, I felt that my integrity was being called into question. Standing up for your principles and values matters far more than a purchase agreement.

If mistakes and setbacks allow for growth, then throughout my sixteen years at the helm of GoodMark's ship I had many 'growth' experiences! A few key business decisions stand out.

As mentioned more than once in this book, at the advice of business and financial consultants, I authorized acquiring two turn-around businesses: a struggling, cash poor trail mix business and a cashless, start-up refrigerated brownie company. While we had turned *Slim Jim* into a profitable business, consultants we hired to make growth recommendations suggested that we diversify our product line to avoid putting all of our eggs into one basket and having 'single product jeopardy.'

Both companies had good products, but we quickly learned that these businesses did not complement our core business; they distracted from it. To make these companies successful would require us to take time and investment capital from the GoodMark brands that we had grown into a commanding market leader. I quickly learned that I authorized a big mistake; we should stick with what we know and avoid distractions with businesses that fall outside of our expertise. Fortunately, we divested these businesses from our portfolio without any significant capital investment or damage to our core brands.

I also gave the go-ahead to purchase a competing meat snack company with lower margin products than ours. Although over time we had taken market share from this competitor, I justified the purchase as an opportunity for us to more quickly grow our business by essentially buying their market share. Was I wrong! I learned that you actually can dilute your business and profitability by adding lower margin (and lower quality) products even if they complement your core business. Sticking to our brands and continuing to grow our own distribution and market share proved a more successful strategy, particularly with our already commanding market leadership position.

As a leader, I also had my fair share of missteps as documented throughout this book. Believing that for GoodMark management and employees to respect me, I had to involve myself in every aspect of our business could quickly have derailed our potential for success. Fortunately, I quickly changed my approach to the betterment of our employees and company.

On occasion, I hired technically qualified, capable people who for personality or leadership style reasons did not fit into our workplace culture. Invariably, both the hire and employees with whom they worked suffered for it. I learned that skills represent only one part of the equation; I tried to lead by example, and encouraged our managers to consider what we now refer to as 'soft skills' as much as 'hard skills' when making a hire.

I could write much more about my mistakes, setbacks and failures along the way - some imposed on me and some self-inflicted. The most important lesson I learned did not come from any business negotiation, staff hire or acquisition. It did not come from anything *external*. It came from what I internalized - and staying true to my beliefs, values and goals despite those that underestimated me along the way.

I simply did not allow negative assessments of my capabilities to diminish my self-esteem. I knew what I could accomplish and achieve given the opportunity.

Sure, the negative comments stung in the moment. As a teenager, walking away from my date's house after her father told me that *a farm boy like me would not amount to anything* was not fun. Believing in yourself and your capabilities - even when others do not - is life's secret sauce. It allows mistakes, setbacks and failures to become springboards for learning leading to success.

If you gain only one valuable lesson from this book, I hope that's the one you remember.

Chapter Eight

ABOUT TEAM WORK

"Hire smart, empower well and get everyone moving in the same direction."

Growing up, the Doggett's worked as a team.

Nothing creates interest and a healthy dose of curiosity like *success.*

At GoodMark, our team took a fledgling company with declining market share and returned it to good health and profitability. People wanted to know: *how did we do it?* Sixteen years after selling GoodMark to ConAgra, I still get asked this question from time-to-time.

Sure, I could recite hundreds of things we implemented to restore our customers' confidence leading to increased sales, profitability and market share. Improving product quality, as an example, certainly made a difference. However, something fundamental had to occur first. Thankfully, I learned it early in my tenure. *Hire smart, empower well, and get everyone moving in the same direction.* This approach became the foundation upon which the GoodMark house was built.

In my view, it was the single most important contributor to our success.

Our marketing strategy after we bought the business from General Mills illustrates this well.

From my perspective, promoting the *Slim Jim* brand when General Mills owned the business for the most part was distribution driven and more reactive than proactive. As I recall, our marketing and selling strategies during those years pretty much boiled down to *if you can get it on the shelf, it will sell.*

As part of our turnaround plan, we became convinced that to grow the business, we needed to become a marketing-driven company with a solid advertising program. This became even more evident because we had excellent distribution numbers, including in 90% of convenience stores nationwide. However, stocking shelves and hoping for the best simply would not accomplish our goals. Jump-starting sluggish sales and getting them moving in the right direction needed much more.

Developing and executing a marketing plan first required hiring smart, and we did just that. We assembled a very talented team of marketing, advertising and public relations professionals, including an experienced marketing president, who filled critical skills gaps.

The old adage *you need to spend money to make money* definitely applied to building our marketing efforts. We invested millions of dollars to hire key talent, sure, but also to conduct research and focus group studies; hire a public relations agency; and develop advertising plans.

With a talented team in place, at their recommendation, consumer research would become the foundation of our efforts. I must admit, at first, the accountant in me worried about the amount of our investment and whether it would produce the desired return.

Hiring smart and empowering our employees paid off in spades.

Research revealed our target customers as males who loved country music; the outdoors; and sports - primarily professional wrestling and auto racing. Armed with this and other market data, our team developed and executed a comprehensive advertising strategy. We hired world champion wrestler, 'Macho Man' Randy Savage, and USA champion stock car driver, Bobby Labonte, as celebrity spokesmen for our advertising campaigns. We sponsored country music groups such as Charlie Daniels, George Strait, Garth Brooks and the Dixie Chicks, and diverse sporting events like NASCAR.

We did not stop there. To create brand recognition, we connected our marketing initiatives to our sales efforts. This included redesigning packaging and in-store merchandising displays to feature our celebrity spokesmen.

With our marketing strategies in place and working, we turned our attention to improving our direct sales approach. Not only did we increase our field sales force, we implemented training to keep our long-standing customers and capture what our marketing research revealed as our new target customers. I loved joining account managers in the field and visiting with customers. Not only did it build loyalty, but customer feedback helped us provide the best products and service possible.

We believed these and other efforts would help significantly grow the *Slim Jim* brand - and boy, did they ever! We grew sales at a compound growth rate of 12% in the sixteen years we owned the business. Although difficult to quantify the direct impact marketing has on sales, I firmly believe that without the efforts of our creative and hard-working marketing team, we simply would not have achieved these results.

How did we get the rest of our employees behind our new marketing strategy? We invited our celebrity spokesmen to our plants and offices to get the GoodMark team knowledgeable and excited about our approach! I could never understand why some leaders try to keep employees separated. I felt just the opposite; the more our employees felt a part of a team and connected to our *whole* business, the higher the morale and the more motivated and productive they would become. I wanted our accounting professionals to hear about marketing successes. I wanted our sales force to know about manufacturing process improvements.

While these efforts contributed to improved sales, profit and relationships externally, creating a 'team' culture *internally* did not come easily.

In the early years after we bought GoodMark, our team made a number of necessary changes. A surgical team, we knew the 'patient' needed a life-saving operation. We had our plates full as we implemented new plans and programs to rebuild the *Slim Jim* brand and make it healthy once again. In a short period of time, in addition to hiring critical employees, we created new broker and distributor relationships; improved the *Slim Jim* formula to increase quality; and changed our hours of operation with overtime expected to get the job done. Some long-term GoodMark employees saw more change in months than they had seen in years. Turning the company around required all to adapt.

Change is never easy. With new employees and expectations, some inevitable human relations issues resulted as we worked to build a new culture. For example, our sales, marketing and manufacturing teams experienced some conflicts particularly as sales and distribution improved. Marketing decided on packaging criteria, not manufacturing or new product development. Sales determined shipping schedules, not the warehouses or plants from where the product would come. Manufacturing dictated how quickly product could ship, which at times frustrated sales.

To get our talented teams to see beyond their areas of responsibility would take some effort. I felt that if we could solve the communication problem, improvement in how our employees worked together would follow. How did we tackle this challenge? We actively created opportunities for leadership and employee interaction.

We formed an Executive Council of senior leaders and a Management Council of department managers, and invited both groups to a two-day retreat that involved equal parts business and social. During the meetings, I encouraged honest communication focused on building relationships and solutions - not just complaining. To illustrate the importance of working together, I referenced the team-building methods used by inspiring coaches including Vince Lombardi, Bobby Knight, Jimmy Valvano, and Dean Smith. No one could argue with the longevity or success of these teams. Quotes from Tom Peters' *In Search of Excellence* and retired General Electric CEO Jack Welch's *Straight from the Gut* frequently punctuated my presentations and discussions.

Post-retreat, I strongly encouraged frequent communication sessions to build inter-department relationships. We received excellent feedback on these discussions and, over time, they produced the desired effect. Morale, confidence, creativity and communication between teams increased. A direct correlation existed between our departments and teams working together and *effectiveness*. Success resulted.

Was our corporate culture perfect? Of course not. Yet, I made it my mission to put in place all the right building blocks for a positive, inspired working environment. Creating an *us* - a team - mentality takes time, commitment and effort. But the return for our business by investing in our people cannot be understated.

It also just makes for a more enjoyable and fun place to work.

Chapter Nine

ABOUT JEANETTE

"I could write an entire book about my wife."

'Then go for it.'

It was early 1982. The lengthy, detailed and sometimes difficult negotiations between General Mills and my team to buy GoodMark finally had resulted in an agreed upon purchase price of $31.5 million. In retrospect, the uphill 'David and Goliath' challenge of persuading General Mills to take us seriously turned out to be the easy part. Securing the financing and accumulating the funds necessary to actually purchase the company would prove formidable to our buy-out team who collectively had limited personal assets.

It also would involve great personal risk for my family and me. To go forward, Jeanette and I would have to use literally all of our assets with cash value toward the purchase. This would mean that we could lose all we had accumulated in our twenty years together; savings, insurance policies, home equity, my prized coin collection, our children's college funds, and our cars all could disappear. *We would put everything on the line.*

It was daunting to consider, and I admit I had a few sleepless nights contemplating the enormity of our impending decision.

The conversation Jeanette and I had the night before our team's final 'go/no go' decision is one that I will never forget. We exhaustively discussed the positives and significant negatives that going forward could mean for our family and way of life. As part of the team acquiring the company, not only could we lose it all, we also would have personal liability for over \$31 million. At the time, we hardly had \$5,000 of equity in our home. Although I could see the brass ring for my professional career within sight, Jeanette and I considered this decision very carefully. We had a new home and considerable financial obligations you would expect with a family of four children. Did the potential rewards override the catastrophic risks? Could we rebuild if the unthinkable occurred?

That evening, I asked Jeanette for what seemed like the thousandth time over the past several months if she *really* supported my acquiring the company. She asked me again and again if I really had the determination, passion and excitement to go forward. I responded with a resounding *yes*. Would I have regrets if I passed up this once-in-a-lifetime opportunity? When I responded *yes* yet again, her four words of encouragement and support *then go for it* sealed the deal. I still remember where we both stood in our kitchen when she uttered those words with such conviction. Together, Jeanette and I went for it. It represents one of many instances throughout our lives together where my wife's support and partnership positively impacted me and our family.

While many spouses would have strongly discouraged or flat-out rejected taking such a risk, my Jeanette is cut from a different cloth. While some may say that she took a big risk giving the green light for my professional adventure, she has made many courageous choices throughout her life to support the people she loves. Jeanette's experiences taught her that life can change in an instant, and this helped to inform her desire to live with no regrets.

Over the years, many have characterized me as an 'entrepreneur.' If truth be told, my wife's can-do spirit, decisiveness, positive attitude, determination and creativity make her the *real* entrepreneur of our family.

Growing up in Austin, Minnesota, Jeanette Reinartz started her life in prison. Well, sort of.

Her father Al's job as the county sheriff meant that her family lived in a house literally attached to the jail. Some of Jeanette's earliest memories included helping her mom, Ruth, cook and serve the prisoners each day. What an education she received! The daily experience with the jail helped to reinforce Jeanette's values, including her strong sense of right and wrong.

Jeanette also felt compassion for some of these men, and learned at an early age that sometimes good people make mistakes.

Jeanette's parents

Jeanette, her sister Sue and brothers Tom, Mike and Dan enjoyed a wonderful childhood as a close family, with a strong Catholic upbringing like my family. Jeanette loved school, and excelled academically and socially. A cheerleader, she had a wide circle of friends and what we called 'suitors' in those days. Atypical of the times, she had a strong desire to go to college and wanted to become a teacher. She loved children, and dreamed of having her own family one day.

Jeanette first learned that life can change quickly when at eighteen years old, her mother died of breast cancer after a lengthy illness. In those days, breast cancer did not have the same level of awareness and support that it does today. She witnessed her mother's declining health, and as a young girl became acutely aware of life's fragility. It made her determined to not take anything or anyone for granted. With her mother's passing, suddenly, she went from the idyllic life of a teenager planning to begin college to a responsible mother figure helping her busy father raise her younger siblings. The few years after her mother's death proved difficult, but she bravely soldiered on and sacrificed her personal desires to provide her family with needed stability. She grew up quickly, and felt her mom's loss acutely. Her selflessness, loyalty, commitment and support for her family would reoccur many times over her life.

Eventually, she fulfilled her dream of going to college. The day she enrolled at Mankato State University became a turning point in her life - and mine. As in high school, she immersed herself in her studies, cheerleading, suitors and a wide circle of friends. Jeanette and I both grew up in Austin, but it would take a chance encounter during our college years at an informal gathering with friends to meet. Jeanette had all the qualities that I hoped to find in my life partner: vivacious, charming, a great sense of humor, friendly, caring, attractive, lively, intelligent and a smile that could light up a room.

Although I was 'smitten' immediately, she did not reciprocate the feelings as she was 'going steady' with another young man. I remained patient and hopeful and, when her relationship ended, I was first in line to ask her out. Over fifty years later, I still remember my elation when she said yes. I wanted her for keeps!

Jeanette had a positive influence on my life right from the beginning of our relationship. I credit my professional success to Jeanette's wisdom and advice. I respect her greatly. Many times throughout our lives together, my wife explained her perspective with love and a healthy dose of conviction and passion when needed. Although we sometimes saw things differently, I respected her opinion and loved that she held her ground. She became my partner and trusted advisor right from our relationship's beginning. We were equals in every sense of the word.

Her words could impact me like no other. One early example stands out. At one point during my sophomore year, I considered dropping out of college to spend more time with my partners on the ill-advised shopping mall venture described in this book. Jeanette listened to my reasoning. She then let me know in the strongest terms possible that while she supported my desire and understood my impatience to start my business career, she disagreed with my dropping out of college. She felt it important that I achieve my goal of getting my college degree so that I would have career options in life.

Needless to say, I stayed in college and graduated. Did Jeanette's advice keep me in college? Absolutely. Did she positively impact my professional career? Without question. My initial opportunity at General Mills simply would not have occurred without that degree.

One of the happiest days of my life occurred during Jeanette's senior year of college and shortly after I accepted my first auditing job with General Mills: we became engaged! The nine months between our engagement and our wedding became a whirlwind, and we hardly saw each other. Work demands required that I travel all over the United States including to California, Oregon, Washington, Idaho, Montana, Texas, Oklahoma and Florida, to complete audits for General Mills. Jeanette finished her senior year of college and planned a wedding, largely without me. I experienced first-hand during this period the wonderful person who would soon permanently share my life. Jeanette supported my long absences and our separation as part of the job and never complained.

After my final audit in Florida, I drove nonstop all night to arrive in Austin just two days before our wedding. On a very hot June 23, 1962, Jeanette became my wife. Our ceremony occurred at Queen of Angels Catholic Church followed by a reception at the Kingswood Inn on the Hormel Family Estate in our hometown of Austin, Minnesota. Jeanette had planned a beautiful day for us to begin our life together, and I could not wait for that life to start.

Our honeymoon began what would become for us a nineteen-month road trip, thanks to my job and company. To avoid long separations from my new wife, I asked General Mills to allow me to become the first company auditor to travel with his spouse. To my surprise, they agreed. Not so surprisingly, my adventurous wife agreed to travel with me. As I had to be in Buffalo, New York nine days after our wedding for my next audit, Jeanette and I had a fantastic time on our honeymoon driving from Austin to Buffalo by way of Canada. We enjoyed many sights along the way, with spending time in Niagara Falls on both the American and Canadian sides a trip highlight.

Jeanette and I took up temporary residency in Toronto, Canada, and traveled all over Canada and the United States to wherever General Mills needed me to conduct company audits. Our travel included New York, Florida, Tennessee, Illinois, Kansas, Oklahoma, Texas, California, Oregon, Washington, Idaho, Montana and North Dakota. We rented apartments and stayed in hotels. In some cities, Jeanette worked as a substitute teacher or did office work at a General Mills location. Our relationship grew and deepened over many conversations in the car from one location to the next.

In Jeanette, I had a fun, adventurous, spirited partner. We thoroughly enjoyed these early, carefree months of our marriage, and eagerly planned for and looked forward to expanding our family.

As my career progressed, Jeanette became my rock. During times of struggle with my work and management aspirations with General Mills, she always encouraged me and frequently offered solutions that made me wonder why I did not think of her excellent suggestions myself! She inspired me to become my very best, and had faith and confidence in my abilities. Once our buy-out of GoodMark became public, when others within General Mills doubted that we could make the company successful, my wife never wavered in her positive attitude and staunch belief in me.

Jeanette loves life, and delights in learning and experiencing. She adores her four children, their spouses and her eleven grandchildren. A fun, happy person by nature, she took great pleasure in her role as President and CEO of the Doggett household where cleanliness and organization ruled. She enjoys a large circle of close friends that expanded over her lifetime, but never contracted. Catholicism, our church and her volunteer work including with the Food Bank and Catholic Parish Outreach gave her immense satisfaction and joy. She enjoys red wine and strong coffee. Golf, tennis and Pilates count among her passions. She loves antiques.

The bravery and support that Jeanette exhibited by telling me to *go for* my professional dreams, pales in comparison to a decision she made in 1975. That year, her brother Tom learned that he needed an urgent kidney transplant. My wife, a mother of four young children, immediately volunteered to donate one of her kidneys to save her brother's life. To go forward, Jeanette faced significant risks. She would undergo major surgery with a lengthy recovery and no guarantee that her brother's body would accept the new organ.

Understanding the risks and obstacles, Jeanette still wanted to help her brother. In those days long before laparoscopic surgical options existed, Jeanette's selflessness would require major surgery with a significant recovery period. I had reservations and concerns for her health but, after a serious discussion, ultimately supported her decision. I admired her bravery even as I worried about her survival and recovery. Sadly, her brother's body rejected Jeanette's donated kidney and he passed away a short time after surgery. Yet, Jeanette lived on knowing that she did everything possible to help a brother she loved.

This selfless, loving act defines my wife and how she has lived her life. I believe this helps to explain why she so willingly allowed me to pursue my dreams; she loves deeply and realizes that things can change in an instant. People and experiences matter so much more to her than possessions and money.

'Then go for it.' While I went for it in business, I really went for it when Jeanette Reinartz agreed to go out with me, become my wife and share my life. Succeeding in having her by my side for over half a century allowed me to succeed in every other way that I went for it.

Whatever path you take in life, picking the right partner makes all the difference.

Jeanette and I start our life together, June 23, 1962

Happy Birthday
JEANETTE!

I love your smile! Best Wishes. My
I love your laugh! best date!
I love your I love your company! You are charming!
you are a Treasure! you are my inspiration!
you are my you are my pride and
support! you are I my love joy! I
I love your, I my there you love your
energy! Love As, Confidence!
you are your pride Mom! you are
Brave! We love your sweet!
you are! Cooking! I love your faith!
a leader! you are a great wife!
you are my True love! you are a
you are my I love great example! you are
"better your Company my best
half!" you are always friend!
you are a helpful!
wonderful I I love your you
Gran'mommy. determination! are
you are the Best Friend! you are loving! you give
Greatest! special us pride!

Happy Birthday
To a great lady, Jeanette!

To Jeanette, from your husband. One of many handmade birthday
cards and poems, and my wife loved them all.

Chapter Ten

ABOUT BEING A GOOD FATHER

"You Only Get One Chance to Raise Your Children Right."

Mark, Anne, Jane and Michael, 1991

Through my professional, community and philanthropic activities, I have received recognition and titles over the years. While humbled and honored, none even come close in importance than my roles as *husband* and *father*. In my heart and mind, then and now, family comes first.

That's not to say that raising four children with Jeanette while balancing a demanding career was easy. Graduating from college, becoming employed by General Mills, marrying Jeanette and having three of our four children all occurred in a quick six years. From early in our marriage, like many families, life in the Doggett household required a considerable amount of juggling. Jeanette and I shared the common goal of wanting to create a similar family life like we had growing up in Minnesota, with fathers who actively participated. We consciously made our family and raising our children a top priority. We worked hard, and had distinct roles and responsibilities. But we worked as a team.

Not uncommon for the 1960's and 1970's, Jeanette had primary responsibility for our home while I worked to provide for our family. Despite my work demands before and after buying GoodMark, I did my very best to attend important events in my children's lives. I wanted them to see by my actions they had a father who participated and cared. Sometimes professional commitments interfered and, at times, I likely disappointed my young children who did not understand their dad's absence. Jeanette and I tried to use such occasions as a teaching opportunity, to explain why Dad works and what that provides for our family.

Yet, I made sure that business obligations - which increased over the years as my career and job responsibilities grew - shared space on my daily calendar with soccer tournaments, swim meets, piano recitals, Indian Guides, Boy Scouts, and ballet performances. As with many parents, I learned to juggle better than most clowns.

In the early years, perhaps because Mark, Anne and Michael came into our lives consecutively over three years, I spent more time with them together than individually. We went places and did things as family. Jeanette and I agreed that unless out-of-town, I would make every effort to have dinner with our family and help get the children ready for bed. Bath time, reading bedtime stories and later, helping with homework, gave me special one-on-one time with each child. I frequently spent several more hours working after they went to bed, but I would not have traded spending that time with my children for anything.

Jane's arrival five years after Michael added both joy and some logistical challenges to our family. It coincided with my career's growth which made my out-of-town travel more frequent. At seven, six, five and newborn, our children had begun to have different activities, interests, playdates and needs; Jeanette frequently did more than her share of the parenting and chauffeuring. I hated when my business travel kept me from our family's nightly rituals or my children's activities. I frequently felt torn. I loved my job *and* my family. How I wish today's technology like e-mail and cell phones - which make staying in touch much easier - existed back then. Daily phone calls helped, but poorly substituted for being at home.

Jeanette and I wanted to instill values in our children through leading by example, rather than preaching, whenever possible. As an example, we did not just tell them to work hard; we wanted to show them. As children who lived very comfortably, taking them with me to work on occasion provided a fantastic teaching opportunity. They could see that my working made our lifestyle possible.

They witnessed first-hand my interactions and conversations with employees, my nice office and my prominent role at company events; achieving the level of *CEO* meant that I had an important job. My sons toured the GoodMark plant with me and not only saw what we produced, but experienced what hard work could accomplish.

They had fun, but Jeanette and I wanted these 'field trips to Dad's office' to provide life lessons as well: through hard work and passion, they could accomplish whatever they wanted in life.

I also wanted my children to see what Dad did while away from them, and to feel a part of it. When Randy Savage or other celebrities who promoted *Slim Jim* visited our offices, I invited my children to meet them. Over time, our family dinners included Jeanette and me telling them about our days and accomplishments. In addition to celebrating their school, sports and other successes, they learned about *ours*. Celebrating the achievements of others became an important value that we tried to instill in our kids.

Working hard at home mattered too. All four children had chores that increased as they got older. Receiving an allowance depended on their successfully completing those tasks! Some of the best times I had with my sons occurred doing projects around the house. My dad could fix just about anything, and passed along some of his skill to me. I hoped to do the same for my sons, and collected a large assortment of tools over the years. My daughters did not have much interest, but I loved showing Mark and Michael how to use them. As we made home repairs or built things like a treehouse or go-carts, they learned how to accomplish through doing to benefit themselves or our family.

It also gave us an opportunity to have wonderful father-son conversations which I cherish to this day. No topic was off-limits and through these unplanned discussions, I frequently learned about their friends, girlfriends, concerns and many other things. I hope that working with hammers, saws and nails taught my sons more than just building or fixing something in the moment; I hope it taught them skills for building their lives.

Like most fathers, my two daughters occupy a special place in my heart. They both participated in a full range of activities, and whether ballet recitals, Girl Scouts, basketball or soccer, I loved cheering them on and celebrating their successes. Mark, Anne and Michael left home for college in rapid succession, leaving Jane at age thirteen an 'only child.' By default given her birth order, Jane received more individual attention from Jeanette and me than her older siblings. During her teenage years, she likely saw this as a blessing and a curse, but Jeanette and I relished spending time with our youngest. We knew when Jane left for college, as empty nesters, our lives would change forever. Jane gave us the opportunity to parent a child for the last time - a role that we greatly loved.

I hope my children treasure their growing up years as much as I do.

Jeanette and I had similar disciplinary styles, although that role frequently fell to her. There was no *wait until your father gets home* in our house. We supported each other; our children learned early that if one parent made a decision, the other would back it up.

We also stood united in wanting our children to grow up with the *Golden Rule* and other values including patriotism, respecting your neighbor, and helping the less fortunate as an expectation. They could recite *do unto others as you would have them do unto you* early in their lives. We tried to reinforce that they would be judged by the company they keep. We wanted them to make education a priority and to receive their college degrees. I told them frequently that an education and our unconditional love are the only things in life that can't be taken away.

Attending church as a family to help instill our faith and values in our children meant a great deal to Jeanette and me. Judging from the people Mark, Anne, Michael and Jane have become, I think we did a pretty good job.

I remember each milestone in my children's lives like it happened yesterday. First steps, first days of school, first communions, first dates, first breakups, learning how to drive, the natural teenage rebellion that each exhibited in their own unique ways, and the list goes on. All left lasting memories. I treasure those moments.

Jeanette and I raised four children with very different personalities, perspectives and strengths. Most important to us, they all share outstanding values; have married well; and have created families and lives for themselves that I respect. They live in close proximity to each other and, with their spouses, have a presence in each other's lives. I admire the adults and parents they have become, and hope they know how proud they have made their mother and me.

During my military service and throughout my business career, the people I admired most had families. They seemed to excel in their personal and professional lives. They demonstrated pride in their family's achievements. I learned a valuable lesson early to not have a career *as* my life, but to make it a *part* of my life. It's a lesson that I gladly pass along.

Mark, Anne, Michael and Jane, I hope you know how much I enjoy being your father and a part of your lives. I love and respect each of you.

Merry Christmas
Ron and Jeanette Doggett and Family

Chapter Eleven

ABOUT FUN

"Start each day expecting to have fun."

My eleven grandchildren mean the world to me.

I enjoy a good practical joke. But whenever I can play a prank or two on good friends *and* promote *Slim Jim* at the same time, it truly makes my day! I still enjoy supporting this product.

During and after my GoodMark years, I became known for greeting friends, family, colleagues and pretty much anyone with a *Slim Jim*, which I kept in ample supply in my pockets. A great way to start a conversation particularly as an ice breaker with someone I did not know, some weeks I gave out dozens. It became my trademark as CEO, and also a great way to market our flagship product. I passionately promoted the brand, and had fun doing it.

Over the twelve years I served on the WakeMed Health & Hospitals board of directors, my fellow board members became accustomed to my signature greeting. But I decided to take it one step further, and our decision to have a retreat in Florida gave me just the opportunity. An unusual decision, as we generally had our off-site meetings much closer to home.

The first evening of the retreat included our team meeting for dinner at a wonderful restaurant. As we relaxed and socialized over cocktails, the waiter announced a special surprise first course, complements of the house. Each of us received a beautiful covered dish, and my colleagues could not wait to see what the chef had prepared. Not only did I pull off a great prank when they learned that a single *Slim Jim* graced their plates, but I enjoyed telling the story for many years to come!

It did not take long for a few of the board members to return the favor. A short while later, they hosted a dinner and completely surprised me by serving ravioli made from *Slim Jim's*. Whatever it takes to make a sale!

When I think about having fun and enjoying my life, simple moments like these fill me with the most gratitude.

Spending time with Jeanette, our children and their families automatically comes under the category of *having fun*. Our family knows how to have a good time together, no matter what the activity. I strongly believe that the family that plays together, stays together.

From the first months of our marriage, Jeanette and I shared a passion for travel, exploring and meeting new people. Even when money was tight, we always found a way to enjoy ourselves. Jeanette's positive attitude and spark for life made everything fun.

What adventures we have had with just the two of us, friends, our children and now with our children's families!

I fondly remember when each of our children learned to ski, and taking skiing vacations together became a highlight of our year. We explored the United States, Canada, the Caribbean and Mexico in planes; trains; riverboats and automobiles; on bicycles; and by foot. A trip we took to the Grand Cayman Islands ranks high on my children's list of favorite family vacations. We wanted our kids to learn about the world; meet people from diverse cultures; and experience different religions and beliefs. Some of the most important education they received about tolerance and respect for others occurred on these trips, particularly when we got off the beaten 'tourist' path. They had a chance to see the world that awaited them as adults. We also wanted them to realize their good fortune to have these experiences.

Jeanette served as the Doggett family travel agent. Her planning skills and attention to detail ensured that we had a fantastic time. It did not matter if our family piled into the car for a local road trip or vacationed in a foreign land; Jeanette thoroughly learned about the history and culture of our destination. Any castle we toured, national park we visited, or famous landmark we enjoyed, Jeanette frequently knew as much if not more than a tour guide. We all soaked in her knowledge, and had a much better time for it.

I feel fortunate that the vacations my family took before my children grew up and created lives for themselves occurred, for the most part, before cell phones and other technology made really 'getting away' obsolete. As much as technology would have helped keep me connected while away from my family during business trips, without it, our vacations gave me the opportunity to talk with my children without distractions. I cherished this time.

The *Most Brave* award in the Doggett family also goes to my wife, hands down. Jeanette was fearless. She climbed pyramids while I stayed behind with my feet firmly planted on level ground because I feared the descent. She gamely swam or floated down underground rivers that I would not enter. She participated in the *Running of the Bulls* in Spain while I watched and prayed for her survival. Thankfully, my prayers were answered!

Some experiences that make me chuckle today came from language barriers during our adventures. One experience proved painful to my wallet, doubly painful for me as I remain fairly thrifty even to this day.

During a trip to Paris, Jeanette, a friend and I arranged to have lunch atop the Eiffel Tower, my treat. The restaurant, a beautiful French-inspired bistro, came complete with professional waiters dressed in formal attire. With the waiter speaking very little English and our command of French limited at best, ordering became an adventure particularly since the menu did not include prices. We had champagne to celebrate with our friend and wonderful French cuisine. While I knew we had just enjoyed an extravagant and expensive meal, when the waiter smiled and presented me with a bill for $475 American dollars ($600 with tip), I could not hide the shocked look on my face. I even asked the waiter if he had given me the correct bill; from his response, I fear that I inadvertently offended him.

I can safely say that was the most expensive lunch I have ever had in my life. Lesson learned. From that day forward, I made sure to avoid sticker shock in foreign countries; you can bet that I knew the price whether pounds, lira, francs or dollars - before buying! Jeanette and I laughed about the experience over the years, which made the price tag almost worth it.

The trip that Jeanette and I took with friends to Africa stands out for many reasons. I find it difficult to put into words the excitement, beauty and, at times, heart-pounding exhilaration of a safari. Having up close and personal encounters with wildlife in their natural habitats; hearing a symphony of sounds that included lions roaring and elephants' trumpeting; and traveling through unfamiliar terrain with only a small jeep to protect us - could not be more different from our day-to-day life in Raleigh. Photographs and videos simply do not capture the experience adequately.

Our travels through Africa and around the globe reminded us of how much we take for granted living in the United States. On some of our trips, the contradiction of seeing and enjoying some of the most beautiful sights the world has to offer against a backdrop of people living in difficult conditions remained with me. While I love to experience new cultures, after each trip I return home with a greater appreciation for, and pride in, being an American.

Jeanette and I always had on our bucket lists a trip to see Christianity's birthplace. We finally made that dream a reality for our 50th wedding anniversary, when we renewed our marriage vows in Jerusalem. What a special trip for us. Although by the time our trip began we knew Jeanette had Alzheimer's, thankfully, its early stage allowed us to enjoy the experience together. We enjoyed seeing and experiencing the places in Israel where Christian, Jewish, and Muslim traditions converge. It also would be the last overseas trip that we would take together. I will never forget it.

Making memories with our grandchildren has allowed 'Grandmommy and Papa' (Jeanette and me) to experience the new and familiar through their youthful, fresh eyes. I felt the same about our children; our family traveling to New York City at Thanksgiving stands out. We enjoyed the Christmas lights in Manhattan, snow covered Central Park, Broadway and the festive holiday spirit in one of the greatest cities in the world. A highlight for Jeanette and me included seeing the annual Macy's Thanksgiving Day parade in person, made special by my children's exuberant laughter.

They delighted in the marching bands, beautiful floats and large helium balloons of their favorite cartoon characters which look so much bigger in person. My children and grandchildren make any activity pure joy.

As much as I love to travel, the everyday experiences that make life fun matter to me the most. For years, our Christmas card has included a photo of our whole family, now numbering twenty-one! When viewed collectively, they beautifully document both our family's growth in numbers and our grandchildren growing up over the years.

Someone once asked me to define *my perfect day*. Without much thought, my answer included a variety of ordinary activities: a big breakfast of eggs, bacon, grits, juice and strong coffee; saying my prayers; reading the newspaper; working in my garden; skeet shooting; an early morning golf game; refinishing some furniture; grilling steaks; enjoying time with Jeanette and our family; a good Manhattan or rich red wine; watching an exciting football game; and enjoying a great book. The simplest pleasures in life give me the most joy.

Leisure activities, hobbies and travel also allow me to recharge my batteries.

Throughout my life, particularly during the challenging 'rebuild' years after we acquired GoodMark, eighty-hour work weeks became the norm. A change of scenery, spending time with loved ones and getting away from work allowed me to return rejuvenated and refreshed. Innovative solutions to complex problems frequently came to me during these times. I learned that taking a break enhances performance. I tried to lead by example, and strongly encouraged our employees to take their vacations. *Work hard, play hard* seems to me a good way to live.

I also tried to mix business with pleasure whenever possible. Golf games with customers, board members and staff allowed relationships to develop which benefitted our business dealings. Our annual GoodMark board and executive staff retreats combined social gatherings with strategic planning. Frequently, our spouses joined us. These events contributed to developing collegiality and important decisions about our company's direction frequently resulted.

Our family loves the beach so much that after fifteen years of renting beach houses, we eventually built our own on Bogue Sound in Emerald Isle, North Carolina in close proximity to the Atlantic Ocean. As my children got married and had their own families, our beach house became a favorite destination for the whole clan to spend precious time together.

Family fun to us means spending as much time as possible outdoors enjoying the salt air and ocean breezes. We have enjoyed countless hours sunbathing, taking long walks on the beach, waterskiing, swimming and collecting seashells.

Catching clams and blue crabs remains a family favorite. I never tire of wading into the Sound waters with my grandchildren and seeing their delight as our digging produces hundreds of clams. Steaming and eating them provides a great reward for our efforts. Blue crabs can be feisty and much more difficult to catch! I enjoy watching my grandchildren scream and run to avoid a crab on the loose as much as I enjoy the crabbing itself. Hauling our catch back to the house; steaming them and making my homemade cocktail sauce; enjoying our feast with a cold beer on our deck; and enjoying the Sound's vastness cap a perfect day.

Sometimes, I have found the solutions to my most difficult business problems at the beach. One such instance occurred when my three partners unexpectedly asked to cash out on their ownership the day after we bought GoodMark from General Mills. This would leave me the surviving owner, with no cash. I truly thought I might lose the company and my dream. The grueling schedule for months of working by day; developing our management buy-out plan by night; and presenting and closing the deal with General Mills had left me badly needing to recharge my batteries.

I decided to go forward with the beach get-away weekend our family had planned to celebrate purchasing the company. I hoped that having some fun in a relaxing, stress-free environment for a few days would allow me to return with solutions and a fresh perspective. It did. I returned to Raleigh rejuvenated with a plan to save the company which proved successful.

Truth be told, my career after we bought GoodMark felt more like a hobby to me than work. How could you *not* have fun when your marketing and advertising featured professional wrestling, auto racing, bull riding and country music! Even with the many challenges, particularly when we first bought the company, I simply loved my job. I took great pride in the organization our team built.

I thoroughly enjoyed spending time in the field, 'the trenches,' with our marketing and sales teams and getting to know our loyal customers. I became known as a 'hugger' and loved surprising our employees throughout the company with unexpected visits.

I could not wait to get to work most days. I wanted our organizational culture to reflect the same attitude, and worked hard with our executive team to create it. I believe you have to really enjoy your work to excel. We wanted our employees to be creative and try fresh ideas to make the company successful. Encouraging fun while working hard helped to promote this.

Winners face life with a positive attitude, enthusiasm and a good sense of humor. To me, *fun* reflects a way of living more important than any activity. I try to enjoy the gift of being alive and vital each day. I plan to continue making fun my daily mindset and a priority for the rest of my life.

At one of my retirement celebrations, 1999. Jeanette and I
looking forward to our future - and many more years of fun.

Chapter Twelve

ABOUT HANDLING ADVERSITY

"At times, I struggle. I am human."

December 2011; after Jeanette's diagnoses,
a difficult year comes to an end.

Everyone experiences ups and downs in life. Career, financial, family and health can present challenges when least expected. I have tried to gracefully accept God's plan for my life and that which I cannot change. I know He has smiled favorably on my family, and I am a very lucky man. Yet, I must admit that sometimes I struggle or ask 'why', particularly when the adversity affects a loved one's health or limits my capabilities.

In the mid-1990's, I developed a tremor in my hands. This ironically coincided with one of the happiest and most satisfying periods of my life; GoodMark continued to thrive as did my family. At first, I ignored it thinking stress and exhaustion were the culprits and wishfully hoped it would go away. But when the shaking progressed to where I neither could write legibly nor give out communion hosts at church, I knew the time had come to seek medical attention.

The diagnosis of Parkinson's Disease, a chronic condition that affects the brain's nerve cells, shocked my family and me. In 1996, research about this crippling disease painted a grim reality, with an average 15% shorter lifespan and a progression that can make walking and talking difficult. My family and I now faced a new normal. As I had throughout my life, I would need to call on my determination yet again to get past the diagnosis and figure out solutions to have the best quality of life possible.

I learned that Parkinson's patients generally die from the disease's complications and not from the disease itself. Once I came to terms with the reality, I made it my mission through exercise, diet, a positive attitude and medications to do everything possible to minimize symptoms and live fully. I assured everyone that I had no intention of slowing down; I planned to get the most out of life with a positive attitude. While I have had to modify some of my activities and have good and bad days, eighteen years later I am still going strong.

Before the Parkinson's diagnosis, I intended to continue running GoodMark indefinitely with no plans to retire. After, my executive team, board and I had to evaluate what would serve our publicly-traded company's best interest. As Chairman, CEO and major shareholder, nothing outweighed my fiduciary responsibility to our investors, customers and employees.

Our team put a comprehensive succession plan in place. Two years later, we merged with ConAgra Foods, Inc. (ConAgra) for a significant return on investment for shareholders and an agreement that preserved opportunities for many of our loyal employees. Many had worked for General Mills and GoodMark for decades; throughout our lengthy negotiations with ConAgra, I cared greatly about doing whatever possible to protect them. I hope they know that I did my very best.

While I know we made the right decision to sell, doing it left me with some mixed emotions. GoodMark had been a part of me for the majority of my adult life. *Slim Jim* felt like a member of my family. Jeanette and I had a fantastic time at my retirement parties, which celebrated the end of one chapter and marked the beginning of my next one. From the lemons of my health challenge, came lemonade. I optimistically looked forward to my future.

Today, I struggle with the drastic change in our family's life brought on by Jeanette's Alzheimer's Disease diagnosis in January 2011. For several months before testing confirmed our worst fears, Jeanette's forgetfulness steadily worsened. Perhaps in denial, but I optimistically hoped that advancing years and a little memory loss would explain the changes. Looking at the photo at this chapter's beginning taken of Jeanette and me nearly a year after her diagnosis, she seemed the picture of health. How outward appearances can deceive.

Alzheimer's is a cruel disease with no cure. Unlike Parkinson's, little can slow down the decline. It robs the afflicted of all memory, while loved ones helplessly can do nothing but provide care. It can produce changes in personality, angry outbursts, physical attacks and other behaviors so uncharacteristic of the person you know so well.

Six months after her Alzheimer's diagnosis, we received another blow when we learned that Jeanette has breast cancer. This diagnosis affected us deeply, particularly Jeanette, who at eighteen years old lost her beloved mother to this disease. Fortunately, the doctors caught her cancer early; since having surgery she has maintained a clean report. Knowing that Alzheimer's would take Jeanette from us soon enough, I was thankful that she did not need chemotherapy or other debilitating treatments that would rob her of her remaining time with us. We lived life fully, and made the most of that time as a family.

Alzheimer's has been referred to as *The Long Goodbye,* and I now understand why. Words cannot express the sadness I feel watching my partner, my love, with whom I shared a life for over fifty years slip away a little more each day. To see Jeanette, who never met a stranger, remembered everyone's name, and lived life at full speed taken from us this way saddens me beyond measure. I know it is what it is; I have accepted her life's plan and our supporting roles in it. Yet, I find myself frequently asking God for strength as I struggle at times with *why.*

I am human.

I emphatically wanted Jeanette to remain in our home for the remainder of her life. As her primary caregiver, I did my very best to meet her needs. Our family did not realize how challenging caring for her would become, particularly as her illness progressed. A sad day for us occurred when we realized that Jeanette needed more round-the-clock care than we could provide. I had a difficult time accepting our decision and the finality of her leaving the home we had shared for decades. I now visit her each day, and am comforted that she receives the professional support and attention she needs. I hate leaving her, yet know it's best for her and our family.

I miss so many things about Jeanette and our life together. Her positive attitude, spark and outlook on life. I think often of her smile, giggle and laugh as we shared stories and jokes. How we traveled all over the world, sharing once-in-a-lifetime experiences while consuming great food and wine. Her passion as we discussed politics, business, government, the economy, health issues, and the fascinating developments in science and technology. How she delighted in her children and grandchildren. Her good judgment as she helped me analyze business problems and come up with solutions. The thousands of times we played tennis and golf or walked on the beach. Her intelligent arguments with the more liberal members of her family entertained her friends and me. Her charming, friendly, kind and loving demeanor made a difference to those who knew her.

I long for our dates, which I looked forward to as much as when we courted. I miss her hugs and kisses. I never will get used to the emptiness in our bed. Life has changed drastically and against my will, but I remain an active participant. I continue to find joy in my church, family, friends and community activities. I feel grateful for my wonderful years with Jeanette, even as I mourn her loss in our lives and the loneliness I feel without her. I remain steadfast in my faith that God has a reason and a plan. That, which I hold onto, gives me hope and comfort.

Jeanette and I intended to spend these years enjoying a full and active life. We talked about trips we would take someday, and things we would do when I scaled back on my community activities and board service. We had a plan, but life made other plans for us. The quick and dramatic changes in our lives brought on by Jeanette's Alzheimer's taught me the importance of living every day to its fullest. We only have today, and what will occur in the future remains a mystery.

I learned that if you really want to do something, find a way to fit it into your life *today*. Do not wait for someday; do it *now*. I remain optimistic, and try to live each and every day fully.

I wish I still had Jeanette by my side.

Chapter Thirteen

ABOUT FAITH

"My faith helped shape my values."

Commercial airliners hijacked by terrorists to kill thousands of innocent people on U.S. soil seemed more likely to occur from a *reel* on a movie screen then in *real* life. I, like many Americans, naively had the false sense of security that terrorism would touch my day-to-day life only through newspaper articles and the nightly news. As horrified as I always felt reading and hearing about suicide bombers, hijacked airplanes and innocent people unnecessarily losing their lives outside of the United States, I never thought it would happen *here*.

That changed forever on September 11, 2001. That day started leisurely for Jeanette and me on vacation in Wyoming with friends. We rose early, and turned on the television in our hotel room to quickly catch the news while getting ready for our full day of fun. With eastern and mountain time zones separated by a few hours, by the time we turned on the television, the terrorist attacks already had occurred and thousands had died on U.S. soil. The surreal images of planes crashing into New York City buildings, the Pentagon and a Pennsylvania field; skyscrapers falling into piles of ash and rubble; first responders in full gear; and New Yorkers fleeing for their lives covered in soot will remain with me for the rest of mine.

It would take days for me to gratefully learn that those I know in the affected areas were not among the thousands that had perished. Months

and years would pass before our lives settled into
what had become a new normal for my family,
friends and our country. But in that moment, I
knew our country would never be the same. I was
reminded yet again that life can change in an
instant. Watching the horrific scene unfold on my
television, Jeanette and I, now joined by our
traveling companions, felt the same uncertainty
and fear about what would happen next surely felt
by all Americans that day. Would the attacks
continue? Would others senselessly die? How would
our country respond? With more questions than
answers, I took comfort in the one thing that has
sustained me in good and bad times throughout my
life.

I prayed.

Religious beliefs are very personal. I include
faith here neither to preach nor sermonize. I have
a great deal of respect for diverse religions, and
have learned much over the years from those who
think differently. Yet, a book about my life and
values would be incomplete without some mention
of how my faith has shaped them.

Growing up Catholic, my earliest memories
include faith's comforting presence in our family's
day-to-day lives. My mother, a devout Catholic
since birth, and my father, who converted to
Catholicism for my mother, shared similar beliefs
about the religious values they wanted to instill in
their children. Despite the long work days to run

our farm, reverence for God and faith-based practices played a prominent role in my family's life. We prayed before meals. 'Don't even think about not going to church on Sunday' could have been our family motto; attendance was mandatory. I vividly recall my First Communion, Catechism, and reciting the Rosary with my parents. Going to Confession (now called Reconciliation) occurred nearly every Saturday.

Like many Catholics, our home prominently displayed a framed photo of the Pope. My mother, in particular, took great comfort from having Pope Pius' presence in our home. Not only did we see his picture, but we heard his voice when as a family we gathered to listen to his weekly address through our only connection to the outside world: the radio. My grandchildren would find it hard to believe that life existed before television and all the technology they take for granted.

I can assure them it did.

Attending Catholic high school, the nuns instilled in me far more than what I learned about chemistry, algebra or religious principles. At the time, my friends and I thought they were tough and sometimes unfair with their high expectations and strict adherence to discipline. Later, I came to appreciate that I learned from them a work ethic and desire for excellence that contributed to my achievement in life.

I owe them a debt of gratitude.

As a child, faith gave me many things including a sense of belonging. But it goes much deeper for me. My faith helped shape my values. One example stands out. Our Minnesota farm community had Lutheran, Methodist and Baptist as dominant faiths, with Catholic in the minority. I sometimes felt discrimination and exclusion, for example, when fathers told me that I could not date their daughters solely on the basis of my faith. This made a big impression on me. As angry as it made me, it taught me the importance of tolerance and respect for all irrespective of their personal beliefs.

In Jeanette, I had a partner who shared my beliefs. We believe that God cares for us and answers our prayers, even though sometimes the answer differs from our request. That provides me with a great deal of comfort. Together, we gave to our children those same beliefs instilled in us by our parents. It gives me great pride to see our children and their spouses continuing that family tradition with their children.

During times of personal or professional difficulty, when something unexpected or drastic happens, my beliefs have sustained me. Rather than lose faith, I intensify my prayer. I ask our church clergy to pray with and for my family and me. Through Jeanette's and my health issues; deaths of friends and family; professional crises; natural parental worry about my children and grandchildren; and many other times in my life as chronicled in this book, I have found support in the church. I also give thanks for the many joys and blessings in my family's life.

Jeanette and I worshiped at St. Francis of Assisi in Raleigh for over thirty years. We loved to go to church together, and became active with our church community including supporting Catholic Parish Outreach and other charities. In 2013, we were so honored when the Catholic Charities of the Diocese of Raleigh presented us with the *Bishop F. Joseph Grossman* Community Service Award. To receive recognition from an institution that has given so much to our family meant the world to us.

Although it saddens me that Jeanette can no longer attend with me, I still go to Mass nearly every week. As the priests along with the altar boys and girls prepare, quite often they will see a devoted parishioner, me, sitting alone in a pew well before others arrive and the service begins.

This opportunity for quiet, solitary reflection has become one of my favorite parts of going to church.

Chapter Fourteen

ABOUT EMPATHY and GIVING BACK

"I feel compelled to serve my community and help develop the next generation of business leaders."

Growing up, I looked forward to Christmas each year. I have wonderful memories that include sledding with my sisters, decorating our Christmas tree, attending Midnight Mass at church on Christmas Eve and opening presents. Even though some years my parents could afford only fruit or cookies for gifts, I barely noticed. My sisters and I appreciated what we did receive. Our family had fun and focused on what really mattered: Jesus' birth and celebrating the holiday together.

Throughout my childhood, I often witnessed my parents' generosity to those less fortunate during Christmas and throughout the year. In our rural community, neighbors helped one another in good and bad times. It's just what we did. My parents did not just say "love your neighbor as yourself," they practiced it. They instilled in my sisters and me the same value of giving provided to them by their parents: no matter how little we had, others needed more. Surviving the Depression combined with their strong faith also contributed to my parents' charitable spirit.

While my parents frequently told my sisters and me how much better it is to give than receive, it was their actions not their words that left a life-long impression on me. Of their many generous acts over the years, one in particular has stayed with me.

As with many communities, ours included several families in need plagued by unemployment, chronic illness, disabilities or other serious life challenges. One family in particular touched my mother's heart when she learned that their home had no running water, heat or indoor plumbing, and the family frequently went hungry. My parents wanted to help them. Our entire family paid them a visit and in a dignified, respectful way, we offered them homemade baked goods made by my sisters and me; clothes sewn by my mother from chicken feed sacks; and simple rock candy prepared from brown sugar. As I looked around their home with no furniture or curtains, I realized that even though our family struggled at times and lacked material possessions, we had much to celebrate.

When I saw the tears of joy and smiles from our gifts, it made me feel good. I felt proud of my parents and our family. We had little to give, but gave what we could. We showed them we cared. That makes all the difference. My parents would help many families this way over the years.

As a child, I remember the steady stream of homeless men who would walk for miles to area farms like ours looking for work. My father became known for hiring these men to help us on our farm in exchange for a meal, a place to sleep, and a tub in which to take a bath and wash their clothes. My father's compassion and the gratitude expressed by the men during their time of need also made a big impression on me.

Our church also reinforced the importance of charity with many programs and services to help our neighbors in need. Our family supported them whenever possible. My upbringing taught me about showing compassion for others. Philanthropy and giving back can make a real difference to our neighbors in need. It also feels good.

Service became a permanent part of my DNA. I feel compelled to share my good fortune with others.

In Jeanette, I had a partner whose parents also instilled in her these same values. As a newly married couple, we wanted our family life to include active participation in our community. We shared a strong desire to raise our children to give back.

Over the years, no matter how busy my career or our family life became, I made time to serve. Board meetings, fundraising events and other community activities shared space on my calendar with other obligations. In addition to supporting our church, I have a special place in my heart for organizations that help children and those in poverty. Jeanette and I included our children in our activities whenever possible.

One example stands out. I became involved with many caring and charitable groups over the years including Habitat for Humanity, a wonderful organization that builds and repairs houses around the world for people in need. One year, our family sponsored building a house. We got a chance to meet and talk with the home's new owners, and my children experienced their gratitude. To see the family's joy as they received the keys to their new home made me very happy. Jeanette and I always felt grateful that we could share our abundance with others.

In every area of my life, I set goals and targets for accomplishment. The same applies to my community service. Perhaps that explains why many organizations have asked me to chair their fundraising committees over the years! I feel very proud that I have worked on teams with talented non-profit staff and business leaders to raise millions of dollars for our community. Knowing that their son has contributed to diverse efforts which have helped thousands of people in need would have made my parents *very* happy.

In addition to charitable work, I also have a passion for mentoring our future generation of business leaders as I was coached so many years ago. In 2000, I was honored to accept an invitation to become an *Executive in Residence* with the N.C. State University business school. This wonderful program helps college students interested in a business career develop through interaction with experienced professionals. Engaging with students through guest lecturing and other activities gives me joy. I hope our time together provides these intelligent young adults - on the brink of beginning their careers - with some value. Judging from their thoughtful questions, they give me confidence that businesses will do great things in the future!

Perhaps my example will encourage them to 'pay it forward' years from now after they achieve their professional dreams. In the not-too-distant future, they will have the important responsibility of inspiring the next generation of business leaders to follow in *their* footsteps.

Sharing my experiences and good fortune with others continues to occupy a prominent part of my life. As a bonus, through community service I have made many friendships and forged business relationships with people who share my values. No material possession can replace the warm feeling that comes from helping someone else achieve their goals or in need. It provides value - an investment - that neither a P&L statement nor an Annual Report to shareholders can measure.

I can't imagine my life without helping others and giving back.

Chapter Fifteen

ABOUT BEING - AND BELIEVING IN - YOURSELF

*"I held my ground, and parted my hair
in the middle."*

This book begins and ends with a story about my dad. It illustrates how I have tried to live my life.

For the reasons explained in this book, I loved and respected my father. As his only son, I wanted to make him proud of me for as long as I could remember. I wanted to be just like him. Since he parted his hair in the middle, as a boy, so did I. The fact that the cool boys at my school (and most other boys for that matter) parted their hair fashionably on the side did not persuade me. My father inspired my hair style and, truth be told, I liked to part my hair in the middle.

No amount of teasing from my friends and classmates could change my opinion. Even as a boy, I marched to the beat of my own drum.

Conforming, even if it goes against what you believe or want, can seem easier at times than staying true to yourself. Peer pressure - whether over how you part your hair, the career path you take, the person you love, the friends with whom you associate, or ideas you support at work - will occur throughout your life.

When news of our desire and intention to buy GoodMark became public, I heard many discouraging and negative voices. I understand. Bucking the norm, doing something unexpected can unnerve people. Some could not imagine taking on the risk. Others thought me unqualified to run a company. Some jokingly (I hope) called me *crazy*. Others flat out said General Mills would never sell to us. Some predicted our demise.

The naysayers made some good points. We did not know for sure the outcome of our bold move. Their comments really projected how they would feel in the situation. We also heard some very positive *you can do it* encouragement as well. I took all the feedback in, but ultimately I listened to the one voice (besides Jeanette's) that mattered: my own. Had I questioned myself on the basis of others' opinions, I would have regretted it for the rest of my life. I did not ignore the risks; I understood the pros and cons and made the best decision for my family and me after careful evaluation.

Buying GoodMark turned out to be a great decision for my career and family's future. Had it gone the other way, I would have figured out a Plan B. Most important, I would have had *no regrets.*

Those that prefer the status quo have existed since the beginning of time. It took a long time for those who believed the world flat to come around. Bucking the expected or advancing new ideas can make people nervous. Each of us has a choice: do we live our lives as others expect or create our own happiness?

I resolved, personally and professionally, to live and define success on my own terms despite conventional wisdom or expectations. My inner compass rarely fails me. When I ignore it, I generally regret it.

As I reflect on my life so far, the ups and downs; successes and setbacks; joys and sorrows, I take great pride that I have stayed true to my core values. I have made decisions right for *me*. I will continue to lead my life that way. I wish that for my grandchildren and anyone reading this book.

We all have one life to live. If given the choice, I hope you march to the beat of your own drum.

Feel free to part your hair anyway *you* want.

Timeline of Selected Meaningful Events

June 15, 1907
> Ron's mother, Inez Cecilia Baldus Doggett born, Story City, Iowa.

December 26, 1907
> Ron's father, Emil Day Doggett born, Appanoose County, Iowa.

June 15, 1931
> Inez Baldus and Emil Doggett married.

December 1934
> Ron born, Austin, Minnesota.

1952
> Ron graduated from Pacelli High School.

January 5, 1955
> Ron enlisted and became a Private, U.S. Army.

October 11, 1956
> Ron honorably discharged, U.S. Army.

Winter 1956
> Ron registered at Austin Community College.

Winter 1956
> Ron involved in a serious car accident returning to Austin from Rochester, Minnesota; hospitalized for several weeks.

Fall 1957
> Ron returns to Austin Community College, Business Administration major.

Fall 1958
> Ron meets Jeanette Reinartz.

Summer 1959
> Ron completes two-year degree; transfers to Mankato State College.

April 1961
> Ron graduates from Mankato State College (Minnesota State University today) with a double major in Economics and Business Administration.

April 1961
> General Mills hires Ron as an Internal Auditor.

August 1961
> Jeanette Reinartz and Ron become engaged.

June 23, 1962
> Jeanette Reinartz and Ron marry, Austin, Minnesota.

November 1964
> Jeanette and Ron's first child, Mark, born.

November 1964
> Ron received first promotion with General Mills; moves family to Chicago.

November 1965

> Jeanette and Ron's second child, Anne, born.

November 1965

> Ron received second promotion with General Mills.

December 1966

> Jeanette and Ron's third child, Michael, born.

August 1967

> Ron accepts position as Vice President and Chief Financial Officer, Slim Jim, Inc. (became GoodMark Foods, Inc.), a division of General Mills; family moves to Philadelphia.

January 1970

> Ron accepts position as Assistant Controller, GoodMark; family moves to Raleigh.

March 1972

> Jeanette and Ron's fourth child, Jane, born.

1972

> Ron promoted to Chief Financial Officer, GoodMark.

Summer 1979, 1980

> Ron attended and graduated from Harvard Business School's Advanced Management Program (AMP).

October 13, 1981

Ron informed that General Mills intends to sell GoodMark.

October 1981-May 1982

Ron leads a four-person team to develop a management buy-out proposal to purchase GoodMark from General Mills.

May 26, 1982

Ron and his team closed on the purchase of GoodMark for $31.5 million in a unique leveraged buy-out. Hawkins Bradley, President and CEO; Ron, Executive Vice President.

May 30, 1982

Effective legal date of GoodMark ownership transfer. Ron and his partners officially owned the company.

May 1982

After acquiring GoodMark, all three of Ron's partners announce their desire to sell the company. One recants, leaving two that want to sell. Ron declines selling the company. Ron negotiates a settlement for his two partners who leave the company.

1983

Ron becomes President and Chief Operating Officer, GoodMark.

1984

GoodMark forms its first Board of Directors.

1985

GoodMark becomes a publicly-traded company; IPO on NASDAQ $10.00/share.

1986

Hawkins Bradley retires; Ron becomes Chairman, President and Chief Executive Officer, GoodMark.

1993

Forbes Magazine recognizes GoodMark as #11 of the 100 Best Small Companies in America.

1993

Ron selected as *Inc Magazine's* Entrepreneur of the Year, Manufacturing.

1993

Ron received the Distinguished Alumnus Achievement Award from Minnesota State University (formerly Mankato State).

1994

Ron receives the GRECA (Greater Raleigh Entrepreneurial Company Award) from the Greater Raleigh Chamber of Commerce.

1998

ConAgra, Inc. purchases GoodMark for nearly $240 million.

1999

Ron receives recognition as the Raleigh Philanthropist of the Year.

1999

Ron receives North Carolina's most prestigious recognition, the Order of the Long Leaf Pine.

July 1999

Ron retires from GoodMark.

2000

Ron selected as an Executive in Residence, College of Management, N.C. State University.

2004

Ron received the North Carolina Hall of Fame business award.

2011

Ron recognized by the Food Bank of Central and Eastern North Carolina.

2013

Jeanette and Ron Doggett receive the Bishop F. Grossman Community Service award from the Catholic Charities, Diocese of Raleigh.

2014

Ron named the 2014 recipient, Greater Raleigh Chamber of Commerce A.E. Finley Distinguished Service Award.

To learn more about Ron Doggett's
Doggett Determination
and for book ordering information,
we invite you to contact the authors at
www.zeldenwritingabsolutely.com.

39392570R00145

Made in the USA
Charleston, SC
06 March 2015